The Timing of Events: Electional Astrology

Bruce Scofield

Astrolabe
PO Box 28, Orleans, MA 02653

Astrolabe, PO Box 28, Orleans, MA 02653

© 1985 by Bruce Scofield. All rights reserved.
Published 1986.
Printed in the United States of America.

91 90 89 88 87   5 4 3 2

Library of Congress Catalog Card Number: 85-73374
ISBN 0-87199-039-3

Contents

1   Introduction

3   Astrology and Daily Life

23   Traditional Electional Astrology

35   Methodology

49   Travel

68   Weddings

84   Business and Employment

114   Further Studies

131   Recapitulation

"Astrological alchemy is the art of envisioning, through planetary symbolism, the realm of possibilities at a particular point in the future and creating through visualization a chosen reality. If your image fits the symbolism well, it will be actualized and you may be spared the possible agony of allowing your conditioning to rule your experience. This exercise of free-will is at the core of electional astrology".

Antipodes Astrologicon

Introduction

In the recent literature of astrology there has been no major effort to update the traditionally accepted rules and procedures for electing a time to commence a project or an event. The existing texts on electional astrology are often very general and offer the reader only guidelines that have been repeated for hundreds of years. There is usually an emphasis on elections based on ephemeral conditions (the current positions of the planets relative to each other) with only a brief mention of other possible orientations. This has steered many astrologers toward basing their judgements on the general ephemeral conditions, not a consistently successful policy in my view. Electional astrology, having been presented only in traditional form, is today somewhat of an anachronism when compared with the numerous developments in the area of natal astrology. This unfortunate situation has led to a general lack of expertise in the selection of favorable times.

Existing texts on electional astrology have two significant weaknesses. Already mentioned is the failure to critically examine the traditional rules. The assumption seems to be that they cannot be wrong since they have been around for so long. It is this kind of thinking that has kept astrology behind the other sciences for hundreds of years. Secondly, there is a lack of case studies. Traditional works on electional astrology have failed to present particular examples, not only of elections, but also of the starting times of natural events.

The Timing of Events: Electional Astrology

The present work attempts to break with this tradition in three ways. First, by suggesting that there may be rules or guidelines other than those handed down for hundreds of years, and second, by presenting actual case studies. Cases of failed events are included since knowledge of what doesn't work can be as valuable as knowledge of that which does. A third departure from tradition is the association of electional astrology with the study of event charts and not with horary astrology, its usual companion.

Electional astrology is for the person who chooses to consciously adjust his reality and hopefully improve it. Correct timing by electional astrology implies a conscious planning of ones life. Ptolemy's *Centiloquy* number 8 reads: "A sagacious mind improves the operation of the heavens, as a skillful farmer, by cultivation, improves nature." Electional astrology is comparable to the use of information provided for us by the weather service. A picnic should be planned for a sunny day; if it appears that rain is indicated, one should dress appropriately or change plans to suit the conditions. The individual who chooses to work with his life and to accept more choice, and hence responsibility, could use astrology to follow the inevitable planetary timing or script more accurately and appropriately, not to diverge from his life pattern for the purpose of demonstrating human willfullness. The emphasis in this book is on personal practical techniques that have the potential of improving our response to the inevitable event-energies that we all must experience. There is no escape in time, but we can get "luckier" and grow as individuals if we dance to its tune. There are many who do not need to use astrology to catch on to this rhythm. Astrology is only one way, a very conscious way.

CHAPTER 1

Astrology and Daily Life

The ability to arrange a personal schedule in such a way that foreseen and unforeseen problems are minimized is a goal that many a person has desired. Timing is everything. It is possible to arrive at something like this through the daily use of astrology provided, of course, that one either has or is a professional astrologer. The ideal situation is when a person is his or her own astrologer because only then can one really know what is actually being experienced in daily life. If one is a careful observer of life and knows a good deal about predictive astrology, then the possibility of maintaining a certain type of control over one's life is greatly increased. This chapter explains how to work with a simple electional system by reading guidelines for one's expectations primarily from transits to the natal chart. This is the cornerstone of personal elective astrology.

As far as most daily events are concerned, an astrological system based on transits is adequate. Directional systems and the very popular secondary progressions have much to say and should provide the background tones for a period, but it is the transits that give daily information and reveal what we might expect to feel like and what may occur on a particular day. Very often directions in particular cannot be reduced to a specific day or even week, and while a major event as symbolized by that direction comes to pass near enough to its exact time to effect a rectification of the birth chart, it cannot be used as an index into the day to day life except as a background tone.

Two formats are suggested in using astrology to gain more perspective over the patterns of daily life. The first is to use lined paper, one line per day, one page per month. Each page is divided into three (or more) columns, the third column being the largest. Directions and progressions are listed in the first two columns and extension lines are drawn indicating their probable range of effect in time. The actual symbols for the aspect are listed on the day that they become mathematically exact. In the third and largest column the transits to the natal chart are listed with transits from the major planets written on the left, also with extension lines indicating their probable range of effect. As you work towards the minor transits, such as those of the Sun, Mercury, and Venus, it pays to make a notation as to whether they are mathematically exact early or late in the day, AM or PM. It is important to note that a minor transit operating during the night when you are sleeping is going to work out in the dream state.

The other method suggested requires that you keep certain long range conditions in mind because they will not show themselves as well as they do on the system outlined above. An ordinary calendar or datebook is used to record the important and not so important transits to the natal chart. This presents problems when several transits and progressions all fall into the same space, or day, on the calendar. Other than this problem of space, this method has the advantage of portability when a datebook is used. There are several very good astrological datebooks available which also include an ephemeris and list the current mundane (ephemeral) aspects and data on a day to day basis. A daily aspectarian can be of great help only after one becomes proficient at reading transits to the natal chart. Ultimately all events are perceived subjectively and it makes good sense to see what is happening astrologically relative to the natal chart and not that of the world. We are talking about personal practical astrology and not mundane astrology.

When all these factors are tabulated, either method should give an overview of the month. With practice you may be able to single out days on which you could expect to experience aggravating conditions and then try to avoid scheduling important events for those dates. The most important factor in doing this kind of astrology is in developing the kind of judgement necessary to correctly appraise a situation and not panic every time that you see Mars square the Sun. The practical astrologer uses astrological guidelines to assist in the goal of having a positive response to the events in his or her life. This is not a way to escape reality but a way to more fully explore it. I might add that this kind of astrology is not for everyone; many do not have the long range vision and self-control necessary for dealing with their lives in this way. Some people should not work with predictive astrology at all; their talents may lie in other areas.

I have stated that the most important factors in a daily practical astrology are transits to the natal chart, but which ones? Obviously transits of the major planets to personal points such as the Sun, Moon, Ascendant, and Midheaven by traditional aspects cannot be ignored. These are going to be background tones like the progressions and directions. Minor transits to the personal points are going to release energies when they tie into a point that is already being stimulated by a major planet. A combination of planets tied into one part of the chart within a few days almost always has enough power to generate an event or at least very strong feelings. Besides transits to the personal points mentioned, transits to the positions of the other planets should be watched also, especially angular planets, the first house ruler, Mercury, Venus, and Mars. After this observe transits to the midpoints of planets and angles that are in some sort of aspect already. Midpoints between planets that are in

6 / The Timing of Events: Electional Astrology

very close aspect, under one degree, should be observed carefully. An example of this would be a semisextile from Mars to the Moon in a natal chart, Mars at 10 degrees Pisces and the Moon at 10 degrees Aries. Twenty five degrees of Pisces, and 25 degrees of the other three mutable signs, becomes a very sensitive point and should be watched carefully.

In order to know the future you must first know the past. If it wasn't so time consuming, pages of rules could be written from which one could read trends from transits to the natal chart in all possible combinations. The problem is that no two charts respond to transits in exactly the same way and such an exercise would have limited worth. What has to be done is a thorough historical search and daily recording of events and subjective impressions and feelings. To regulate your schedule more effectively you must invest time in reviewing the past and its astrological correspondences to your life. You should keep some kind of diary to record the daily experiences along with the astrological factors, all for future reference. If you notice that every time the Sun passes over a certain planet in your chart a similar feeling or event takes place, then you have a basis on which to make an accurate evaluation of a day in the future. If you happen to notice, and a good observer will, that certain events or feelings seem to coincide with the passage of a planet over a certain degree of the zodiac, and the square and opposition to that point, you may through experience discover a zone of great sensitivity. This zone, or more accurately degree, may turn out to be a midpoint between two planets, a point which completes a natal planetary picture, or perhaps even the progressed position of a natal planet.

In this kind of astrology fixed rules are impossible. Robert Hand's book *Planets in Transit* is as good as you can get but it can only explain how the transits operate in a general context. It is up to each person to look into his or her past and correlate it with transits, backed up with progressions or other long range predictive techniques, to the natal chart.

One quick method of locating when a transiting planet contacts (aspects) any sensitive point in the natal chart is to construct a sensitive point catalog or listing. This is a listing, for each sign of the zodiac, of the exact degree and minute that constitutes an aspect to a natal point. This is a very helpful exercise for persons who have initial problems with astrological geometry and many of my students have benefited from both the exercise of doing it and the product itself. A sign by sign listing of many minor and micro aspects to a natal chart can help considerably in the understanding of these usually overlooked aspects — overlooked due to their difficulty of calculation. Computer midpoint sorts, now readily available, are also extremely useful for this kind of work. I have found the 45 degree sort to be particularly helpful.

Another assignment I have given to students who are learning to work with predictive astrology is worth mentioning also. First the student is asked to select what are considered to be the major events in his or her life for the past five to ten years and to investigate the planetary configurations relative to the natal chart at that time. I next ask the student to locate the times when major planets were forming the basic conjunction, square, and opposition aspects to sensitive points in the natal chart. This dual approach to organizing past personal experience usually points out that many beneficial events often coincide with hard (traditionally bad) aspects. This knowledge on a personal basis will, hopefully, alleviate any unnecessary worry about an up-coming hard transit. It also shows how important events have complex structures and that an isolated square will often only coincide with a subjective state and constitute a different kind of event than the student had previously considered. Subjective states can, but do not have to, generate objective events. A historical investigation of this nature often points out very clearly where the most sensitive points in the natal chart are because they will turn out to be transited most frequently at the time of major events.

Judging the quality of an event scheduled for a day in the future during which a transit or two is forming can be highly useful in adjusting one's expectations and in preparing for the day. However, making this judgement can be extemely difficult if there are several transits operating at the same time, each of a different nature. Often an operating progression or direction will indicate the general trend of events and assist in making an accurate evaluation. If this isn't the case then judgement must proceed cautiously. First a transit from a major planet will tend to have precedence over the affair and a transit to a personal point will also be dominant. Transits from major planets that are not mathematically exact on that day but are near to it must also be taken into account, especially those from Saturn which sometimes take days before effects become obvious. The important point is to separate the dominant transits from those that will play only a minor role in the course of the day. The basic aspects of conjunction, square, and opposition are going to have a more direct and challenging impact on the nature of the day and those transits must be studied closely on that account even if they are not aspecting a personal point. It is the nature of these three basic aspects to operate more in terms of events and outer conditions, and more decisively so, than the trine or sextile. Attempting to explain how to make a proper evaluation of probable conditions on a day in the future borders on the futile. My position is that a thorough personal historical investigation is the prerequisite, and that daily observation with the help of a good book on transits is the best route to solid judgement.

There are problems that go along with the practical use of astrology in your life such as the basic problem of living with foreknowledge. The great danger is that you are not emotionally prepared for events in the distant future, events that you may be quite prepared for by the time that you get to them. Another problem is obsession with trying to predict the possible outcome of a major planetary configuration in great detail. Do not waste time in specifying individual events. You must learn to deal with future transits, progressions, and directions as types of energy and general conditions that will become apparent when you get to them in time. You must look at these conditions as neither good nor bad but as just what they are, conditions. You should look at an approaching aspect in a rational manner and ask yourself what types of events would be appropriate at this time and what types would not. If you have no definite plans for a certain period, and you see some powerful aspects forming at that time, you would be wise to try and schedule something appropriate for that period. It is my belief that you can "burn off" some of the negative characteristics of a Mars transit by acting out the more positive characteristics. I generally try to plan some physical activities (sports, chopping wood, etc.) when Mars is acting strongly on my chart rather than waiting around for possible aggravations.

In order to clarify some of the preceding statements concerning aspects or angular distances between transiting planets and natal planets, the following classification is presented. Based on personal experience, this classification is meant to serve as a guideline only and not as a final word on the subject. Until massive statistical studies are done, each astrological practitioner should approach the subject with a questioning mind. The aspects can be divided into three major categories based on strength or power. There are major, minor, and micro aspects. A division of each of these three basic categories results in a sorting of aspects into hard, soft, and variable according to their effect. The hard aspects are those derived from a division of the full 360 degree circle by the numbers 2, 4, 8, and 16. The soft aspects stem from a division of the circle by 3, 5, 6, 9, and 10, while the variable aspects result from a division by 1, 7, 12, and 24. The parallel and the so-called contra-parallel are not distinguished from each other and are classified as variable. It should be noted that the parallel, unlike the other aspects, is a measurement based not on astronomical longitude but on declination.

Major aspects

Hard: Square, opposition

Soft: Sextile, trine

Variable: Conjunction, parallel

Minor aspects

Hard: Semisquare, sesquiquadrate

Soft: Quintile, bi-quintile

Variable: Semisextile, quincunx, septile series (51.43 degrees). The bi-septile, 2/7ths or 102.86 degrees, seems to be the most difficult of the series. It often indicates situations out of control.

Micro aspects

Hard: Semi-semisquare or semi-octile (22.5 degree series)

Soft: Novile (40 degree series), decile (36 degree series)

Variable: 15 degree series. 7/24ths or 105 degrees seems to be the strongest of the series. It appears to indicate a difficult start but a smooth finish. Because it is midway between the square and the trine, Charles Jayne has called it the "squine."

The transiting planets themselves can be divided into two main groups based on strength and power. The planets from the Sun out to the Asteroid belt, including the Earth's Moon, are considered minor, in terms of usual transiting effect, while those from Jupiter to Pluto are considered major. The actual speed (daily motion) of a planet seems to be the best indicator of its range of effect in time and accordingly the inner planets are more potent when near a station and moving very slowly. Following are some observations about possible uses of each planet along the lines discussed in this chapter.

Moon: Transits of the Moon are useful when it is necessary to plan events to the hour. A lunar transit will only last for an hour or two and if you are sure about a very favorable zone or degree area in your chart, you may want to utilize the transit of the Moon over this degree. This applies in reverse to negative zones. The Moon often brings about a minor fluctuation of personal reality most often in the form of a mood swing. The Moon entering the first house often ushers in a few days of strong personal feelings and marks a good time to begin projects that require personal presence, unless the Ascendant is afflicted. Generally, transits of the Moon through areas of the natal chart occupied by many planets will indicate those days during the month when significant activity is likely to occur, or when events quicken.

Besides its transits to the natal chart, the Moon has a general condition which might be considered in personal planning. When, during its motion through any sign, the Moon completes its last major aspect to any of the other transiting planets, it is said to be void-of-course until it leaves that sign. Actions begun during this period are liable to drift or sway from their original purpose —

which may be desirable in some cases. If you want your actions to follow a designated plan, start them when the Moon is not void of course.

Mercury: Transits of Mercury are the next fastest transits and usually last for about half a day. When Mercury is near a stationary point, it can be moving very slowly and has a more pronounced effect often lasting a week or more when aspecting a sensitive area in the natal chart. Mercury transits are useful when communication is an important part of the day's business. A strong trine from Mercury to the personal points makes for clear communication and fewer misunderstandings, unless these points are afflicted in the natal chart, or transiting Mercury itself is afflicted. Squares and oppositions of Mercury to personal points usually indicate problem potential but are not inappropriate to matters that require constructive efforts.

Mercury retrogrades three times a year. If, during the course of its retrogradation, it aspects an important part of the natal chart its effect is especially potent. This is because this point or planet will have been aspected three times by Mercury during the full course of the retrograde sequence which consists of a first aspect, a retrograde aspect and a final direct motion aspect. The issues or matters symbolized by the natal point or planet must be re-thought or re-worked during this triple transit. Completion is usually reached when Mercury passes its first station. Also, issues or matters symbolized by the natal house that Mercury retrogrades in should be re-thought and re-worked. If Mercury stations directly on a natal point or planet, the above description applies but the effects are extremely powerful and tend to dominate the life at that time. Often a retrograde Mercury will appear to be the cause of communication and transportation problems when its stationary points are tied in closely to the natal chart. Just the presence of a stationary point in the zodiacal sign of a personal point is often enough to disrupt the functioning of that point. Do the appropriate under Mercury retrograde — re-work, re-think, re-write and re-trace.

Mercury transits to natal Mars, and Mars transits to natal Mercury, are often symbolic of mechanical work or anything involving the use of the hands. I have learned not to do any major automotive repairs myself when these planets are not configured well as the tendency to abrasion and error is much greater. Driving and traveling are also ruled by Mercury and if you have any indications that you may encounter problems in motion, or that there may be a problem with your car, a hard aspect from Mercury could mean the possibility of problems. I've found that hard aspects of Mercury to Neptune could mean problems with gas, Mercury to Uranus electrical problems, and Mercury to Saturn problems with the brakes. This astro-auto symbolism also applies when the major planets aspect Mercury and also third house symbols. When a problem first appears, note the transits at that time involving Mercury or third house symbols, as this may aid in diagnosis.

Venus: This planet has much to do with social encounters and its transits often give good indications of what a social event may be like. This applies also to transits to the natal Venus. In general, squares and oppositions often indicate conditions that are either boring or somewhat uncomfortable while trines and sextiles are more often pleasant. Venus transiting one of the personal points often makes one popular or attractive to other persons, especially transits to the Ascendant, unless these points are badly afflicted in the natal chart or transiting Venus is afflicted. It is in this kind of situation that an aspectarian can be useful, but if transiting Venus is afflicted by another transiting planet, and this Venus is aspecting a natal personal point, then the other planet must also be afflicting the natal personal point. If you concentrate on transits to your natal chart, you should be able to catch these things without using an aspectarian.

Parties and other social events are best planned to occur when Venus is favorably aspecting the natal chart of the host or party giver. Venus transiting through the fifth or eleventh house is often a good general indicator as to when a social event could be planned. The choice of the exact day would then depend on transits of Venus to the personal points or other important planets and, of course, transits from other planets to the natal Venus.

Venus is also a significator of artistry and it is practical to perform, record music, or paint pictures when the natal chart has strong Venus activity indicated. Musical or stage performance in particular is closely related to the current transiting planets, the best events often involve transits of, and transits to, Mercury, Venus, and Neptune. These three planets linked together seem to be the best indication of high level artistic creativity.

Sun: The transit of the Sun over a sensitive point in the natal chart often brings things symbolized by that point to a more prominent level. The transiting Sun is often the element in a series of planetary transits that marks symbolic turning points and as such is held in high regard by Uranian astrologers as a key factor in predictive work. As the transit of the Sun in hard aspect to planets in the natal chart can often indicate a problem with those in authority, it is generally not advisable to schedule an interview for a job when the transiting Sun is square to the natal Saturn or Midheaven, unless there are other indications to the contrary. Solar transits are of about the same length as a Venus transit, about one day, but even here a simple calculation can determine the exact time of transit which is most often the part of the day during which the event-energies symbolized by the transit occur. Favorable aspects, including the quintile, from the Sun to the natal Ascendant are helpful when planning to make favorable impressions on other people and it pays to schedule important meetings or interviews when these aspects are in progress.

Mars: Very often the impact of a Mars transit will occur shortly before the aspect is technically exact. This is in keeping with this planet's impetuous nature. Its effect usually lasts about two days with the exception of transits to the personal points by major aspect at which times it may have an effect for several days. Transits of Mars to the Sun have their best outlet in the form of physical activity. This could also be said of the Ascendant to a lesser degree, but the Ascendant also implies the general environment including other persons. It is generally best to postpone a tense confrontation with someone when Mars is in exact hard aspect with sensitive points in the natal chart, unless you want a fight or a settlement based on power. Mars square to natal Venus in particular is often not the best time to schedule an important meeting unless the nature of the meeting fits the symbolism of the aspect. It is also common for fevers or sore body parts to develop around the time of a hard aspect from Mars to the natal chart. A favorable transit of Mars to the Sun or Ascendant can be very helpful in events where personal power is a desired factor. Mars transiting the Ascendant, especially in conjunction, often gives the person a strong sense of confidence which is projected to others as a kind of power. This can be useful in challenging situations both personal and social. Transits of Mars are also suited to outdoor activity and especially so when Jupiter is also involved.

Asteroids: The asteroids Ceres, Pallas, Juno, and Vesta, and also the much slower moving planetoid Chiron, although physically small have a definite relation to the events of daily life when they transit sensitive points in the chart. It is suggested that their transits be limited to major transits to personal points. They may prove to be very useful indicators of trends to persons who have them strongly positioned in their natal charts.

Jupiter: From here on we are dealing with planets that define days, weeks, and even months rather than hours of influence. It is still very important to note the exact day that a major planet makes an aspect to the natal chart because its effect is usually noticeable on that day. The typical Jupiter transit, by major aspect to one of the personal points, will usually last about a week or two evenly spread around its mathematically exact aspect. It inspires one to grow and to seek wider horizons. Negatively it can simply make one restless. It is the most important transit to consider when making a major move in life because it offers growth with protection. The transits of Jupiter are especially good for relocations and trips because it tends to promote natural transition. Of course this will not be the case with a Jupiter transit to a personal point that is severely afflicted, though even then it will considerably tone down the negative factors. Major Jupiter transits to the natal chart can be used in planning vacations. A solid transit of Jupiter is also favorable for beginning an educational program or for publishing. Events that involve many persons are best planned for Jupiter transits. The only negative side of this planet is that under certain conditions it tends to produce excesses that can be annoying and it often produces over-optimism.

Saturn: This planet's effect, when contacting a major sensitive point by major aspect, usually begins to be felt seriously about a week after it is exact and may last for the next month or so with a peak at about the third week. If Saturn will retrograde over the aspected point again in a few months you may expect its tone to run continuously for several months and sometimes nearly a year. I have noticed that on the day that the transit of Saturn becomes exact, a minor, or seemingly minor, event occurs that is symbolic of the whole series of events that may unfold in the next few weeks. Long range projects involving responsibility are best begun when Saturn is favorably aspecting a personal point. Many projects which were failures in some way were observed to have been initiated while transiting Saturn was square the natal Midheaven or Sun. The opposition is not as difficult and often marks major decision points in life which may lead to major events. With a strong natal Saturn, hard aspects may not be so troublesome and they may be regarded as a valuable constructive challenge.

Uranus: This is the most impressive transiting planet in its mathematically exact release of event energies. Its transits can be used to rectify charts. Uranus tends to bring about unstable conditions which can have positive or negative implications depending on your flexibility and the quality of your response. Squares and oppositions are to be watched carefully for future scheduling as these tend to disrupt the status quo quite dramatically. This applies whether actual planning occurs under this transit or the planned event is to occur when it is near exact. Avoid marriage while Uranus is making a square to a personal point unless the natal chart shows that this is appropriate. Unusual events such as spontaneous parties can often be very successful under a transit of Uranus, even the hard aspects. Artistic events are often brought to genius levels when this planet is prominent by transit. Its range of effect is about two weeks unless it is moving very slowly and will retrograde over the sensitive point aspected. The proper expectation one should have about a major Uranus transit is that during its passage over the particular natal point, ordinary reality will be disrupted and matters may become quite unstable, but not necessarily unpleasant.

Neptune: This planet's transits are extremely subtle and often cannot be perceived objectively for several months after exactness. Neptune ushers in gradual breakdown and alteration of personal reality and beliefs when aspecting personal points, a situation far more profound than most suspect at the time. Soft aspects are good for making plans for the future, for artistic performances and general creativity, and for doing spiritual work. Generally speaking, avoid investments when Neptune is aspecting anything connected to the second or eighth house by hard aspect. Transits of Neptune to the Ascendant by hard aspect are often dangerous for serious relationships, and if commitment is an issue, the situation should be examined carefully for any unrealistic or deceptive elements.

Pluto: The transits of Pluto are very profound and usually of lasting consequence. Decisive changes in life direction will proceed directly if undertaken around the time of a major Pluto transit to one of the personal points, the appropriate personal point for the type of event. The hard aspects are difficult and it is not advisable to enter into a new personal or social reality at this time unless the natal chart indicates that this would be appropriate or necessary. Transits of Pluto will often mark the times when major turning points are reached, and correspondingly, the times when major decisions and changes are appropriate. Transits of Pluto, and transits to Pluto, are appropriate for activities that probe and explore and also for renovations and restoration work.

Trans-Neptunian Planets: The effect of a transit of one of these slow moving points (they may not be planets at all) is to mark periods in the life like the visible outer planets. They also seem to act very specifically on the days that they form an exact aspect with a natal planet or sensitive point.

Besides the transits of the planets themselves, transits of the midpoints of the various planetary combinations are useful and often explain why a particular event, not indicated by the transiting planets themselves, has occurred. A midpoint ephemeris has recently become available.

In summing up this chapter, a set of aphorisms relevant to daily personal elective astrology are presented in the hope that they may clarify some of the complexities inherent in this approach.

1. Know how to do what you want to do. Good aspects do not solve problems, they only insure a lack of obstacles.

2. Always plan appropriate events under appropriate conditions as indicated by transits to the natal chart. Follow the script and don't try to avoid an inevitable crisis. Meeting hard aspects is an important part of living.

3. Keep accurate records of days that positive and negative events occurred. Analyze this information and use it when planning for the future.

4. When making important decisions for future scheduling be sure to first select a good day to make these decisions. Favorable aspects from transiting Mercury to Jupiter, Saturn, or the Sun are generally good indicators of stable judgements.

5. You will generally have less control over events that occur under hard and difficult transits than those that are soft and favorable. Plan important events for soft and favorable aspects unless the particular event is better symbolized by hard aspects.

6. Days on which no aspects from transiting planets to

natal planets occur are often good days to schedule projects. This condition could indicate that there will be no significant "tides" to fight or move with. Be sure that you are not overlooking anything, particularly slow moving planetary transits exact within a week or two, which become activated by a transit of the Moon or a transiting midpoint.

7. Locate the most exact favorable planetary configuration in the natal chart. Favorable transiting aspects to well placed, exact natal planetary patterns can be frequently used to advantage for numerous activities.

8. Cut or style hair when transiting Venus is in soft aspect to natal Sun, Mars, or the Ascendant, or the reverse-Sun and Mars to natal Venus and Ascendant. The transiting Moon entering the first house is also good for cutting hair and attending to other personal matters.

9. Advertise for buying or selling when the ruler of the second house is applying to a personal point or to planets in the second house. If the ruler of the second house aspects a personal point and is stationary at this point, then retrogrades, matters will not proceed smoothly until this first stationary point is passed, although matters will begin to improve when the planet moves forward again. This general concept will apply to other areas of the life.

10. Sporting events and outdoor activities are best planned to occur when the transiting Sun, Mars, and Jupiter aspect these same points in the natal chart.

11. Begin new personal initiatives when the Sun, Mars, or Jupiter cross over or favorably aspect the natal Ascendant. If the natal Ascendant is afflicted you may experience problems in regard to physical and social interaction with the environment, but these should not be so

severe as your personal power should be somewhat higher than usual.

12. Generally, the best time to buy clothes is when Venus forms soft aspects to the natal Sun and Ascendant and the Moon is in the first house. This rule, like any other general rule, will not apply equally to everyone so it is advisable to keep accurate records of shopping experiences in order to discover your best aspects. This may take a year or more as there may be several combinations worth analyzing. These favorable natal points or zones can become emphasized when progressed or directed planets are near.

13. Plan to entertain or be entertained when natal fifth and eleventh house symbols are favorably aspected. Hard and negative transits to fifth house symbols could mean problems with the enjoyment of something.

14. Watch the motion of the ruler of the house symbolizing the thing that you want to do. When it is favorably applying to a personal point, not afflicting anything else and free from affliction from other planets, make your move.

15. When two transiting planets aspect each other and these same two were in aspect at your birth you will experience "effects" symbolized by those two planets. For example, a person with a Venus — Uranus opposition at birth would be sensitive to any major interaction of transiting Venus and transiting Uranus. This person should not plan a formal business meeting when transiting Venus is square to transiting Uranus. It does not matter where in the zodiac this occurs, but if it does occur on a natal sensitive point the "effects" are powerful.

16. A transit, progression or direction to a natal sensitive point defines a moment in time when subjective reality

tends to be strongly influenced and often dominated by the world of ideas symbolized by the aspecting planet and the point aspected. Thoughts and thought-created events at this time will bring with them into the future the qualities of that moment.

CHAPTER 2

Traditional Electional Astrology

Traditionally, astrological writers have linked electional astrology with horary astrology. This book will associate only event charts with elections, thus breaking the traditional link with horary. This is not to say that horary techniques applied in reverse cannot create a viable electional chart, in many cases they are enough. But I would argue that the "horary in reverse" approach can be limiting because there are many solutions in the elective process, including some that the astrologer in his efforts to follow the rules may never consider. The enormous variety of combinations in natal charts which "produce" personal success suggests the need for wide horizons in electional astrology.

Event and electional charts can be directed and progressed and they respond to transits like any natal chart, with the obvious necessity of modifying meanings. The difference between the event and the electional chart is that the later is the chart of the birth of a consciously selected event. There is a factor of human intervention here that limits spontaneity. This factor can help or hinder an event depending on the skillfullness of the astrological practitioner.

From Graeco-Roman times through the 17th century electional astrology was one of the most actively practiced branches of astrology. Nine aphorisms in the Centiloquy erroneously attributed to Ptolemy pertain to elections and reveal considerable sophistication in this area even in classical times. In considering this ancient heritage we should remember that the destruction of the great libraries of the ancient world meant that only the more popular, and hence widespread, works would survive and be available to future generations. The astrology of Medieval and Renaissance Europe was historically based on a relatively few surviving classical works plus additions and modifications by the great Arab astrologers. It is probable that we have inherited an electional tradition which was developed largely by Arab astrologers who in turn may have used relatively few classical works as a starting point.

Today, the most readily available source of traditional rules and procedures for electing a time are to be found in Vivien Robson's *Electional Astrology* first published in 1937. In many respects, Robson's book continues the traditional format for writings on electional astrology. A comparison with William Ramesey's book on elections (Book 3 in *Astrology Restored*, 1653) shows few differences both in content and organization. Other readily available sources are the article on elections found in the *Encyclopedia of Astrology* by Nicholas deVore, the Church of Light booklet #92 (in *Horary Astrology*), and A.J. Pearce's *Textbook of Astrology*. Noel Tyl in *Analysis and Prediction* and Barbara Watters in *Horary Astrology and the Judgement of Events* also have something to say on the subject.

In his book *Electional Astrology*, Robson points out very clearly that there are basically three types of elections: radical, mundane, and ephemeral or horary. Radical elections are those in which the radix (natal chart) of the person or persons involved in the event is the primary starting points. This kind of electional approach is emphasized in this book. Mundane elections are elections based on references to the preceding mundane charts for ingresses, eclipses, conjunctions, and lunations. If the degree of an eclipse or conjunction is well aspected in an electional chart, it is presumed that the election assumes more than immediate characteristics and becomes a part of the ongoing march of social reality. For example, long term business or political projects might be referred to the degree of the previous Jupiter/Saturn conjunction. William Ramesey specified reference to the chart for the Sun's passage into Aries in all electional work. According to him, if the Ascendant and its ruler in an electional chart were unfortunate in the chart of this ingress, the matter would fail. The use of mundane data in electional work will be considered in a later chapter.

Horary or ephemeral elections are based on the position of the planets at the time of the event with no reference to the radix or mundane charts. Mundane factors and ephemeral or horary factors must guide electional work if the planned event involves many persons or if the birth data of the person or persons involved is unknown. Almanacs that list favorable times for projects and events are based on this kind of data and have a general applicability for the general public. Ephemeral elections make up the bulk of Robson's book and the reader is referred to him for rules and considerations when utilizing this approach.

The following is an overview of the principles of traditional electional astrology. This is not intended to represent a complete synthesis of the astrological past in this field, but is simply an overview of the most widely held general considerations for electing a chart for any kind of event or project. The one rule that most authors seem to agree on is that the natal or radical chart of the person or persons involved should be the central starting point. In other words, most authors favor radical elections. According to Ramesey, when the birth time is unknown the time of the question asked in regard to an election should be used as if it were a radical chart.

Directions, progressions, and transits affecting the native reveal the current conditions effective at the time of the election, and if these are unfavorable, no election will alter these conditions significantly. Primacy of the natal chart also means that in the electional process an effort should be made to avoid negative stimulation of any natal problem areas, particularly those that are symbolic of the project at hand.

Primary consideration of the nature of the natal chart in itself and in time makes good sense. The basic point of electional astrology is to catch that moment in which a kind of opportunistic balance is forming between the person and his near future experience and environment. This should be a moment in which the potential for successful entrance into a new region of experience, padded and ripe with possibilities for growth and success, is high. This kind of information is only available from the natal chart. If a future event is to be meaningful in a positive way to the person who will be experiencing it, then the electional chart should be compatible with the natal chart. If the event is for two or more people, then it should relate in some favorable way to both of them and even to the composite chart of the persons involved. Assurance of this condition is possible only with reference to natal charts.

Probably second to the consideration of the natal chart or radix, there seems to be a general agreement on the importance of the condition of the Moon at the time of the election. It is most often written that the Moon in an election should always be increasing in light, that is to say that one must consider the phase angle of the Moon to the Sun and pay special attention to certain angles. The square and opposition points of the Sun/Moon cycle are to be avoided and it is desirable to have the Moon waxing, that is increasing in light or simply in the first half of the cycle. The point is to start an event before the climax represented by the full Moon and to also avoid the crisis and adjustment points indicated by the first quarter. The project theoretically will then unfold towards fulfillment. The period after full Moon is said to be appropriate for underground or hidden projects such as the planting of root crops. Personal experience seems to indicate that having the Sun and Moon in any close aspect is not necessarily all bad in an election unless other factors come into play and make the tie between the two more stressful. The Sun and Moon linked suggests definite form. It is also possible that lunar rhythms are less influential in modern daily life than in earlier times.

It is also traditionally accepted that the Moon should not be void of course and should be swift in motion. The Moon is void of course when it is past its last major (Ptolemaic) aspect before entering a new sign. A void of course Moon implies a lack of direction, a condition which is said to deny fruition. This seems to be relevant in my experience, though I question the exclusion of some of the minor aspects such as the semi- and sesquisquare which may be serious contenders for first class status. I suspect that it is the change of sign itself (the Moon's transit of the last degree or two of a sign) which is most important in this kind of situation. A slow Moon is said to act like a retrograde Moon, that is it creates a situation in which the affair seems to have difficulties in overcoming obstacles. The Moon should also be free from serious affliction and not be placed in an angular house unless it is very well aspected. Presumably this avoidance of angularity reduces the sensitivity of the event to its environment and consequently its capacity to respond inappropriately. It is important for most elected events to influence, not be influenced.

In *Astrology Restored*, William Ramesey notes ten conditions in which the Moon could be considered impaired or hindered. These are as follows:

1. When in combust with the Sun
2. When in 3 degrees of Scorpio (its fall)
3. When in opposition to the Sun
4. When in square or opposition to Mars or Saturn
5. Within 12 degrees of its node
6. When in the last degrees of a sign and near Mars and Saturn
7. When in the via combusta (15 degrees Libra to 15 Scorpio)
8. When in the signs Capricorn, Aries, or Libra
9. When it is slow in motion
10. When it is void of course

Ramesey also suggests that the lunar mansions and the lunar aspects be considered in an election. He presents two tables (also contained in Robson's book with only slight modifications in the language) which he says were thought worthy of note by ancient authors. The lunar mansions are a 28 sign zodiac, each mansion being equivalent to the Moon's average daily motion. There is confusion as to exactly how they were originally used and also to where in the solar zodiac these divisions began. The lunar mansions may be tied to the sidereal zodiac causing them to change position over time.

Lunar aspects for use in elections are well known and form the basis of most daily guides available to the general public. This kind of information makes generally good sense but probably should not be allowed to dominate an election unless the aspects are exact to within one half of a degree. The Moon in a traditionally unfavorable aspect, off by several degrees, might also be exactly positioned in a very favorable midpoint which could conceivably tip the scales in a better direction.

Other considerations in traditional electional astrology are generally thought to be secondary in importance to the special attention given to the radix and the Moon. Ramesey suggests that along with the condition of the Moon, the planetary significator of the event and the house signifying the event should have priority over other considerations such as the nature of the Ascendant and its ruler. In many instances, experience seems to indicate that is probably correct. The planetary significator and the appropriate house appear to be tremendously important and as such are discussed in the chapters on specific kinds of elections. However, the relative weight of any one consideration is questionable. Perhaps no one set of fixed rules can be applied to all elections because it is the chart as a whole that is most important. With this in mind, the following considerations are probably best seen as equal in importance and to be applied as best as is possible within the context of the preliminary judgements.

The sign on the Ascendant, its ruler, and the planet that best signifies the project or event (the significator) should be strong and free from affliction. The Ascendant is said to be more favorable when ahead of the natal Ascendant, or moved clockwise against the houses of the natal chart, for then as time advances from the start of the event, this Ascendant moves ahead to join the natal Ascendant. The concept of setting up a situation in which things proceed forward as time passes is obviously a desirable feature in most elections. An electional chart should not be set up in such a way that afflictions from transiting or progressed planets occur immediately after the event begins. The ruler of the Ascendant should be in direct motion and in favorable relation to the matter, that is the indicators of the matter in terms of planet, house, and house ruler. The planetary significator of the matter should also be in direct motion.

The signs on the cusps of the angles are important in that they are said to give an indication of the speed in which an event is brought through time. Cardinal signs prominent indicate rapid change and progress, fixed signs denote stability and endurance, and mutable signs favor adjustments and adaptations. The fifteenth degree of the fixed signs are said to be the most stable regions of the zodiac. The importance of this area has been noted in modern times by the Hamburg School of Astrology and its American offshoot, the Uranian System, because of its 45 degree or 8th harmonic relationship to the Cardinal points (zero degrees of Aries, Cancer, Libra, and Capricorn) which constitute the framework of the tropical zodiac. In traditional horary astrology, a chart is said to be void when the Ascendant is changing signs, that is between the last three degrees of one sign and the first three of the next. Experience in studying human behavior has suggested that these transitions are felt by most people and that they do mark natural points of change. Unless an important natal point is located in this cuspal range, or a particular planet located there is to be used in the election, it is better to avoid these degrees entirely. If this range is unavoidable, start the project after the sign has changed. Of course an election for a transitional situation would appropriately have the late degrees of a sign on the Ascendant. This information should also apply to the degree of the Midheaven, particularly in business elections.

The so-called malefic planets (Mars, Saturn, and sometimes Uranus and Neptune) that are severely weakened by affliction, sign, or retrogradation should not be placed in a prominent part of the electional chart such as in an angular house. This makes good sense because the areas near the angles are the most readily expressed zones of the chart and anything here that is not functioning at top performance will only make things worse. Conversely, a favorable planetary situation should be brought out as much as is possible and the custom of placing a "good" planet on an angle would seem to be a good policy. The studies of Michel Gauquelin suggest that planets near the angles, more particularly just after the angles and into the cadent houses, seem to be the most significant planets for at least what he was measuring; planets and vocation, heredity, and personality. It should also be mentioned that Ptolemy stated that the Ascendant began five degrees above the horizon and not at the cusp of the first house. Personal experience indicates that the placing of Jupiter on or near one of the angles (and this includes into the 12th, 9th, 6th, and 3rd houses) in an electional chart tends to produce, or be correlated with, satisfactory and relatively trouble-free events.

A publication called *Valliere's Natural Cycles Almanac* (available from Astro-Graphics Services, Inc.) contains graphs from which the times that the planets are near the angles for any day of the year can be read. The times that Jupiter is rising, culminating, setting, and at the I.C. (and also at the East and West points or equatorial Ascendant and Descendant) are shaded in grey and represent the most favorable times for initiating a project or an event. A successful electional system could begin with the selection of a good day based on transits to the natal chart and then the selection of a good approximate time from the *Natural Cycles Almanac*. I have experimented with this simple method when rushed and have never failed to get good results. With the *Natural Cycles Almanac* you are given a rather large range of time in which to begin an event. Perhaps this range serves to relax the mind and allow it to intuitively select a better instant than the one at which the planet used (usually Jupiter) is exactly on the angle.

Other traditional considerations such as planetary hours, number symbolism, and particular segments of the zodiac merit some attention. Planetary hours, which are related to the seven day planetary week which we all use, are very ancient. The assumption here is that the seven visible planets have influence over segments of time on a rotating basis. In many respects, planetary hours are something of a zodiac in time. Experience indicates that there may be something to them.

Number symbolism (the number of the day, the number of the sign, etc.) plays an important role in Hindu electional systems. This kind of approach is typical of a pre-modern culture but it seems out of place today, which is not to say that it doesn't work. Other aspects of Hindu electional technique, such as the locations of negative or positive areas of the zodiac, should be tested for possible use but there may be major difficulties here due to precession. A zone said to be detrimental may really have been so centuries ago, but as the vernal point shifts against the constellations the original reasons for such a determination becomes lost. This reasoning is also appropriate for dealing with the via combusta, or 15 degrees Libra to 15 degrees Scorpio, a zone of bad fortune passed on to us from antiquity. Again how this came to be is uncertain, it may have originally been the sign Scorpio or the eighth part of the ecliptic starting from the equinox many centuries ago.

To sum up then, the traditional rules for electing a chart for the commencement of an event are roughly the following:

1. Consideration of the radix, or charts of the persons involved.
2. Consideration of the position of the Moon and its condition.
3. Consideration of the condition of the Ascendant, its ruler, and the planets and houses ruling the matter.
4. Consideration of the signs on the angles.
5. Consideration of the positions of favorable and unfavorable planets: emphasize by angularity the

favorable planets and de-emphasize the unfavorable planets.
6. Consideration of the general mundane and ephemeral conditions in effect.

To determine if any traditional considerations were apparent in practice a large number of charts for events, both elected and natural, were examined. This exercise led to the following observations. Whether the Moon was increasing or decreasing in light seemed to make no noticable difference in the charts of journeys or short projects. Charts of successful weddings and businesses (not electional charts) however, more frequently occurred during the first or increasing half of the soli-lunar cycle. Hard aspects between the Sun and Moon, including the semi- and sesquisquare, occurred in the charts of many successful journeys. Many disasters showed trines and sextiles between these bodies. The house position of the Moon appeared to be very important. Travel charts of failures or disappointments often had a first or tenth house Moon. Most good trips had a cadent or succedent lunar house position. Perhaps the Moon prominent makes the trip too responsive to its environment. This suggests that if the Moon is to be prominent in an election, it had better be well aspected.

The condition and house position of the ruler of the Ascendant appeared to also be very significant, especially if it was located in the house or houses that signified the event. An afflicted Ascendant ruler in the third or ninth houses of a travel chart generally coincided with a difficult and disappointing trip. Mercury retrograde consistently coincided with problems on journeys but Mercury combust or in hard aspect to other planets was not a decisive indicator one way or the other. One of the most general observations was that angular placements of the Sun, Venus, and Jupiter tended toward good experiences while Mars, Saturn, and Uranus angular tended towards problems. A chart with the Sun, Venus, and Jupiter all in angular houses, with Saturn, Mars, and Uranus in succeedent or cadent houses, consistently coincided with a good experience. Proximity to the angle itself seemed to make no difference.

In closing this chapter, a comment on exactly what constitutes the beginning of an event is relevant. In the chapters that follow further refinements will be made but essentially in all cases we are looking for the time at which the event becomes irreversible, or passes from potential into the actual. This moment, which is controversial in an event such as a marriage ceremony, is the actual birth of the event itself. Careful observation of events, large or small, in daily life will give one a sense of where these decisive moments are located in time. An analysis of birth times of events will help to direct one to a successful conscious guidance of life's many important starting points or initiations.

CHAPTER 3

Methodology

It is my contention, and that of many astrologers, that the consistent use of a system in the interpretation of astrological data is the best approach. Reliance on intuition is too risky when working with the practical kind of astrology discussed in this book. This is not meant to reduce psychic aids in interpretation to a lower level, but to emphasize the need for regularity in the working method. It is suggested that the evaluation of an electional chart or the chart of a natural event, in the first stages of analysis, begin with the following.

1. Examination of any planets within five degrees of any angle or in close aspect to any angle.

2. Examination of the Sun and Moon, their relationship and their house locations.

3. Examination of aspects to the Sun and Moon.

4. Examination of the significator of the election or event and the appropriate houses and their rulers.

5. Examination of the sign on the Ascendant and the location of its ruler.

6. Examination of any exact (under one degree) aspects and any stelliums.

7. Examination of parallels of declination,

particularly to the Ascendant and Midheaven, for any further information.

The second stage of analysis utilizes an outer circle which is designed for a 90 degree dial or disc. This is the level in which details are dealt with, but only after reconsideration of the dominant configurations. On this chart the Moon's node, hypothetical planets, asteroids, etc., could be included. Certain midpoints such as those involving the personal points should be marked off. Other factors, such as antiscions, might be better kept in mind rather than written down in order to keep the inevitable clutter to a minimum. Using the 90 degree dial the following elements are checked.

1. The nature of the particular day itself is studied with the pointer on the Aries mark. The basic configurations of the day are evaluated and then checked for connections (or possible connections if electing) to the Sun, Moon, and angles. Favorable symmetry around the Aries point is a good indicator of success in a general sense and is of special value in elections that involve the general public. An example would be the Moon and Jupiter equidistant from the Aries point (an indication of popularity) in an election for a restaurant.

2. The significator of the matter is examined in more detail.

3. Since a semisquare or a sesquiquadrate show up as an opposition on the 90 degree dial, the chart is checked for any of these aspects that may have been overlooked in previous analysis. Also check for 22½ degree aspects within 30 minutes of arc.

4. The midpoints of dominant planets and angles, and the midpoints of planets in very close aspect, are

examined.

5. Symmetrical groupings (planetary pictures) of planets are located and their relationships or possible relationships to the angles, the significator, or dominant planets are evaluated.

Analysis on the 90 degree dial emphasizes the second harmonic and its derivatives, 4, 8, and 16. These are the harmonics related to the manifestation of objective events. Use of the 90 degree dial and the examination of planetary pictures is quite complex and the reader is referred to other works on the subject such as *The Language of Uranian Astrology* by Roger Jacobson. It is important to note that this suggested system, with the exception of the parallels of declination, is an astrological system based on the zodiacal longitudes of the planets. Future astrologers may use several kinds of charts in their work in order to arrive at a more complete picture of the planetary relations at any particular point in time. A minority of astrologers are doing this today, but it may take some time for these newer approaches to astrology to filter down to the level of the general practitioner. Hopefully the astrological community will not resist such innovations which are so desperately needed in the astrological field.

To summarize, the method of analysis suggested consists of two basic stages. In the first, the event chart or electional chart is examined in the traditional manner. Seven steps have been suggested, but this is up to individual discretion. A good sense of the main issues in the chart is critical at this stage. In the second stage additional factors and more complex planetary structures are examined on the 90 degree dial. Symmetrical configurations are isolated for special consideration.

A few comments about predictive work with event

charts are appropriate. All natal techniques work with event charts including solar and lunar returns. For long range projects, directions and progressions would be useful along with transits. For shorter events such as trips, the use of transits is usually sufficient. The use of the daily transiting Meridian is particularly useful for short lived events. The Meridian, or Midheaven, travels 361 degrees in one day and thus moves ahead in the event chart at the rate of approximately one degree per day. When this MC contacts or aspects planets in the event chart, "event-energies" are released. This applies to the daily transiting Ascendant also which has a daily motion that varies considerably depending on latitude.

Electional Procedure: Selecting the Best Moment by Stages.

This procedure is specifically for the selection of the best time to begin a project when there are relatively few people involved and their birth charts are known. Since the introduction of the composite chart into popular practice several years ago, it is possible to use that chart as a reference point when two or more persons are involved. It should be used as a secondary factor since the composite describes the relationship as an entity in itself. In most cases an election is made for one person, except in a marriage, and the following procedures will be oriented towards the use of a single natal chart as the starting point for a successful selection of the best moment.

Step one: Select a favorable day to work on the election. Good aspects to natal Mercury and third/ninth house symbols are important. Judgement must be at its best when electing a time.

Step two: Determine which planet is the significator of

the event or project and which house or houses are important. Decide what conditions would be appropriate. For example, consider a wedding. Venus would be the chief significator of the event, the seventh house and its ruler important, and if stability was a desired feature, then the orientation in the selective process (election) would be towards stability factors, such as a fixed sign emphasis or a well placed Saturn. It is most important to know what you want at this stage of the process in order to keep the necessary trial and error maneuvers to a minimum. As a general rule the planet Jupiter can be used as prominent factor in any election because it tends toward success and opportunity.

Step three: Outline carefully the directions, progressions, and transits (and anything else you might use for predictive purposes) and arrange this data in such a way that you can see at a glance when configurations in the various systems are forming close to each other in time. This has already been described in chapter one. This time-graph should cover a sufficiently long period for the matter under consideration, three months for a summer vacation and a year or more for a wedding. Remember that we are all bound by some conventions and this severely limits the possibilities of grasping that "better moment". When this guide is set up, carefully circle or note in some way the periods when crisis, change, and tension are minimal, and also when stable aspects occur. Always look for the appropriate symbolism of the planned event. Pay attention to how the significator is aspected.

Directed or progressed aspects between the personal points represent basic personal developments, and if the event is to be an important one, it should probably fall close to one of these periods. It is generally better to avoid directional or progressed linkages with afflicted personal points. When using Solar Arc directions in either longitude or right ascension, personal points will come together in various ways. The use of one half and double the basic arc, and the use of these measures both forwards and backwards in the zodiac, creates many possible combinations. Secondary progressions calculated for this time-graph should include both progressed to natal and progressed to progressed aspects. Finally, eclipses, lunations and the transits of the major planets, Jupiter through Pluto, should be considered in the selection of a favorable period. A series of lunations or eclipses occurring on a sensitive point in a natal chart can indicate that an important event symbolized by that point is due, hence appropriate for that time.

A general understanding of how the transiting planets are relating to themselves (the ephemeral conditions) during the period in question is also necessary at this point. The significator should be forming good aspects with the other planets. It should not be afflicted at the time of the event unless you really know what you are doing and welcome the challenge. Following the condition of the significator through the ephemeris, along with knowledge of general "good and bad" periods in a persons life based on the above material, is the most rapid way of locating favorable points in time for an election. Transiting planets in aspect with each other that tie into the natal chart in some way are important. An example would be the midpoint of a Saturn-Uranus square passing over the degree of the natal Ascendant, generally not a good time to have a wedding—but perhaps a good time for a divorce. Attention to the preceding considerations should give one a complete overview of the period in which a trouble-free and hopefully successful zone might be located for the event or project contemplated.

Step four: Isolate the most favorable zone or zones, usually a period of two weeks to a month, based on the following criteria.

a. If the event is to be an important event in the life, there should be an aspect forming in the natal chart within a month or two by direction or progression between two or more of the personal points, between the ruler of the first house and a personal point, or between a personal point and the significator (or ruler of the significant house) of the event. Generally this will be a conjunction or one of the soft aspects. If the event is not to be a major event in the life, then this step is not so important.

b. Periods when appropriate (expressing relevant symbolism) transiting planets form trines, sextiles, quintiles, and unafflicted conjunctions and parallels to the natal chart are generally good, safe periods to start something. Favorable aspects of Jupiter to the significator of the event in the natal chart are especially valuable. Frequently an opposition would be a good indicator but this depends on that particular natal chart and the nature of the event.

c. Consider the various aspects forming among the planets themselves at this time, especially those that involve the significator of the event. Distinguish between applying and separating ephemeral aspects as this knowledge can be put to use in an election. Avoid electing a time where an applying hard aspect between planets would close by progression or direction immediately after the event's birth. Avoid creating a "time-bomb."

Step five: Narrow the zone to several days based on convention (the days allowable in your schedule) and on the basis of the transits of the Sun, Moon, Mercury,

Venus, and Mars to the natal chart. Especially note if any of these bodies are favorably aspecting the parts of the chart stimulated by the larger transiting bodies, progressions, or directions. The ideal situation is when a major transit, say Jupiter trine the natal Sun, gets some help from transiting Venus which may be conjunct, trine, or sextile the natal Sun. The basic idea is to locate favorable zones that become re-emphasized.

Step six: With only a few days in focus, try casting rough test charts for each day for a time when a transiting planet that is favorably aspecting the natal chart is on an angle, preferably the Ascendant or the Midheaven. A 360 degree dial or disc is useful at this stage. At this point the electional process is very difficult and it is the purpose of the case studies to suggest how a final judgement might be made. Remember that if you have gotten this far and you are not sure about what to do next, use the *Natural Cycles Almanac* and start your project during a shaded zone. Another possibility is to arrange things so that the Ascendant or the Midheaven of the electional chart is conjunct or in good aspect to natal Jupiter or a known natal success area. These points should be determined by observation and past experience. The following possibilities are recommended in electional fine tuning, though bear in mind that only on rare occasions will all of them be present.

1. Arrange a time when Jupiter is on an angle.

2. Place the significator of the project or event on an angle, well aspected.

3. Arrange some kind of symmetry around the angles, such as having the Midheaven or Ascendant positioned at the midpoint of a Mercury-Jupiter trine for a long journey.

4. Place the Ascendant or Midheaven in the same degree of a planet in the natal chart, one that has something to do with the event and one that is well aspected in the natal chart.

In order to find when a planet or degree becomes angular, simply use a table of houses to determine the sidereal time correlated to when the degree in question is on the Midheaven or Ascendant. Proceed to cast the chart backwards to arrive at the local clock time. See the end of this chapter for step by step rules and example.

Step seven: As a final check it is suggested that a composite chart derived from the election and the person involved in the project be calculated. While this technique has not been thoroughly tested, there are many indications that it may be the best single check available. Any serious incompatibilities will show up clearly in the composite. As has been suggested throughout this book, a historical approach, in this case a study of past event-person composite charts, is necessary for sound judgement.

Hopefully these steps give a fairly good idea of how to narrow the field for a final choice. There are many things in astrology that cannot be reduced to rules that will work consistently. This attempt to explain and outline the system used in the case studies of elected events should have two effects on the reader. First, it will give the reader a background for the case studies. Secondly, it presents an example of a workable system, one out of many certainly, but perhaps more eclectic than most and one that may interest persons who feel caught in the middle of traditional astrology and the German systems which are becoming more popular. Today it is important that astrological methodologies be in constant flux and that a constant search for better techniques be sustained. However, one should also be aware of the need for an organized system at any one point. A simple system is better than many techniques and no consistent application.

Method for Timing a Planet's Angularity

To find the clock time at which a planet is exactly on an angle, measured in zodiacal longitude, and using a midnight ephemeris: Example: Jupiter is at 26 degrees of Gemini and I want a chart that has Jupiter at the Midheaven.

1. Find the sidereal time when 26 degrees of Gemini is at the MC from a table of houses.

2. Add to this sidereal time the longitude time equivalent of your location; this then equals the sidereal time + GMT + acceleration.

3. Subtract the sidereal time for the day (add 24 hours to your figure if the sidereal time of the day is greater than your figure).

4. Divide this figure by 6.1 and subtract this dividend from the original number. This accounts for acceleration.

5. Subtract the time zone difference from the remaining number and you will have the standard time of day (expressed in 24 hours) that Jupiter will be at the MC.

Worked Example

1. Jupiter is at 26 degrees of Gemini. Sidereal time when 26 degrees Gemini is at MC = 5h 42m 34s.

2. Add longitude time equivalent for New York City: +4h 55m 48s = 9h 97m 82s.

3. Subtract sidereal time for the day (3/3/78, midnight at Greenwich = 10h 41m 40s). An adjustment is necessary, add 24 to the figure at step 2. (33h 97m 82s) − (10h 41m 40s) = 23h 56m 42s.

4. Divide by 6.1 and subtract. This is easily done on a calculator; (42/60 + 56/60 + 23) divided by 6.1 = 3m 55s. (23h 56m 42s) − (3m 55s) = 23h 52m 47s.

5. Subtract time zone. 23h 52m 47s − 5h = 18h 52m 47s.

6. Answer is 18 hours, 52 minutes, and 47 seconds of clock time from midnight or 6:52:47 PM EST.

This procedure can also be used to time the passage of a degree over the MC or horizon that is the degree of a body or angle of the natal chart. The horizon and MC at birth, if unafflicted, can be duplicated in the electional chart which creates a kind of new birth chart, same angles but new planets. Other .possible combinations are natal Ascendant degree on electional MC, or natal MC on electional Ascendant. This kind of procedure, that is placing the natal angles in prominent positions, or the "best" natal planet's degree on one of the angles, should be considered at the focusing stage in the electional process as a possible alternative to placing the "best" transiting planet on an angle. Both approaches have given good results in my judgement and constitute the final stages of what is essentially a trial and error situation.

A planet exactly conjunct the Ascendant or Descendant is only bodily on the horizon if its latitude is zero. In many cases there can be a significant difference between a planet's real position in the sky and its position on a standard ecliptic based astrological chart. The actual physical rising of a planet was of considerable importance in ancient Mesopotamian astrology and it may prove to have great significance in electional work. For those who are interested, the procedure for making this determination is as follows.

To Find if a Planet is Physically (Bodily) on the Horizon.

1. Determine the oblique ascension (O. A.) of the Ascendant or the oblique descension (O. D.) of the Descendant.

   RAMC + 90 = O. A. of Ascendant
   RAMC + 90 = O. D. of Descendant

2. Take the planet in question and calculate its O. A. If its O. A. equals the O. A. of the Ascendant, or its O. D. equals the O. D. of the Descendant, then it is on the horizon.

   a. Determine the R. A. of the planet from an ephemeris or from the following formula (which is not reliable when the longitude is near 0 or 180 degrees).

      1. F = arc tan (tan latitude ÷ sin longitude)

      2. R. A. = arc tan [cos (F = obliquity) × (tan longitude)] ÷ cos F†

---

† It may be necessary to add 180 to obtain the correct R. A. which can be recognized because it is always in the general vicinity, numerically, of the absolute longitude.

b. Find the planets ascensional difference (A. D.). A. D. = arc sin (tan declination × tan geo. latitude)

c. Find the planets oblique ascension or descension.

O. A. = R. A. − A. D.
O. D. = R. A. + A. D.

Example: In chart #8, pages 92 and 93, is Pluto bodily on the horizon?

1. RAMC 107.3625 + 90 = 197.3625 = O. A. of the Ascendant.

2. Pluto data:

   a. longitude = 194.08
      latitude = +16.98
      declination = +10.11
      right ascension (R. A.) = 199.56
      geo. latitude = 40.21

   b. A. D. = 8.6695

   c. O. A. = 199.56 − 8.6695 = 190.89

The O. A. of Pluto does not equal the O. A. of the Ascendant, therefore it is not bodily on the horizon. Contrary to what the standard ecliptic based chart would suggest, it is above the horizon. To find a time that Pluto would be bodily on the horizon you would need the O. A. of the Ascendant to equal 190.89, or an RAMC of 100.89 which is equivalent to an MC of 10 degrees of Cancer and an Ascendant of 8 degrees and 40 minutes of Libra. This rather large difference between astrological chart position and true physical position is significant only when the body in question has a high latitude. Pluto is far more critical in this respect than the other planets.

CHAPTER 4

Travel

It is the area of travel that I have researched most extensively. I travel frequently, recording all pertinent astrological data, and have also collected numerous departure times from friends and relatives for my files. This chapter will begin with an examination of the several charts of one trip that was considered by the travelers to be a disaster, the chief problems being uncertainty of direction, and financial and transportion limitations.

My friend Dennis and his brother recently traveled to Ireland for a month and were kind enough to keep an accurate account of departure times and the times of important events on the trip. This case is a good illustration of how a travel chart can respond to transits and it is also an example of a trip with multiple starting times, two of which turn out to be significant. It is also a good example of what not to do in an election for a journey. I have analyzed the trip in the following way.

My friend carefully noted the time he left his house, the time the plane left the airport, the arrival at Shannon airport, the time they left Ireland, and the time they walked back into their house. I cast charts for all these beginnings and endings, taking special notice of the first three charts, the ones that should show the events of the trip. I next listed each event that was noted in my friends diary by the date, time, event description, and positions of the Midheaven, Ascendant, Moon, Sun, Mercury, Venus, and Mars for that moment. Seventeen events were recorded. The next task was to determine if there

The Timing of Events: Electional Astrology

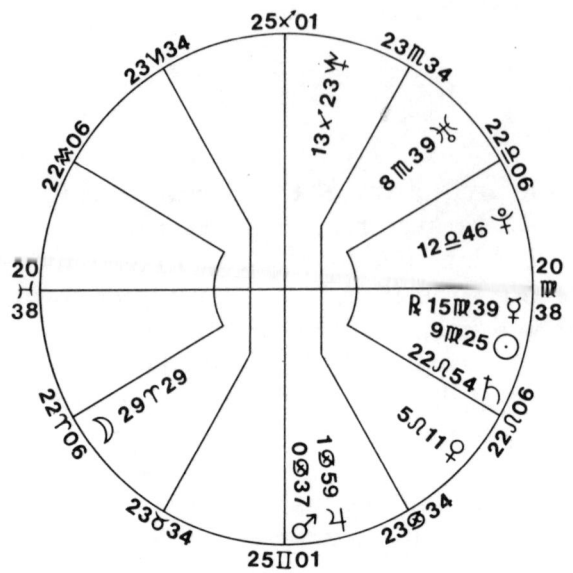

Chart 1 A

	Longitude	Latitude	Right Ascension	Declination
Sun	9°VI25'	0°N00'	160° 59'	8°N02'
Moon	29°AR29'	1°S15'	27° 52'	10°N08'
Mercury	15°VI39' ℞	4°S19'	165° 07'	1°N40'
Venus	5°LE11'	0°S07'	127° 31'	18°N52'
Mars	0°CN37'	0°N03'	90° 41'	23°N30'
Jupiter	1°CN59' ℞	0°S24'	92° 09'	23°N02'
Saturn	22°LE54'	1°N03'	145° 36'	14°N52'
Uranus	8°SC39'	0°N24'	216° 24'	14°S00'
Neptune	13°SG23'	1°N29'	252° 11'	20°S57'
Pluto	12°LI46'	16°N36'	198° 14'	10°N15'

Travel / 51

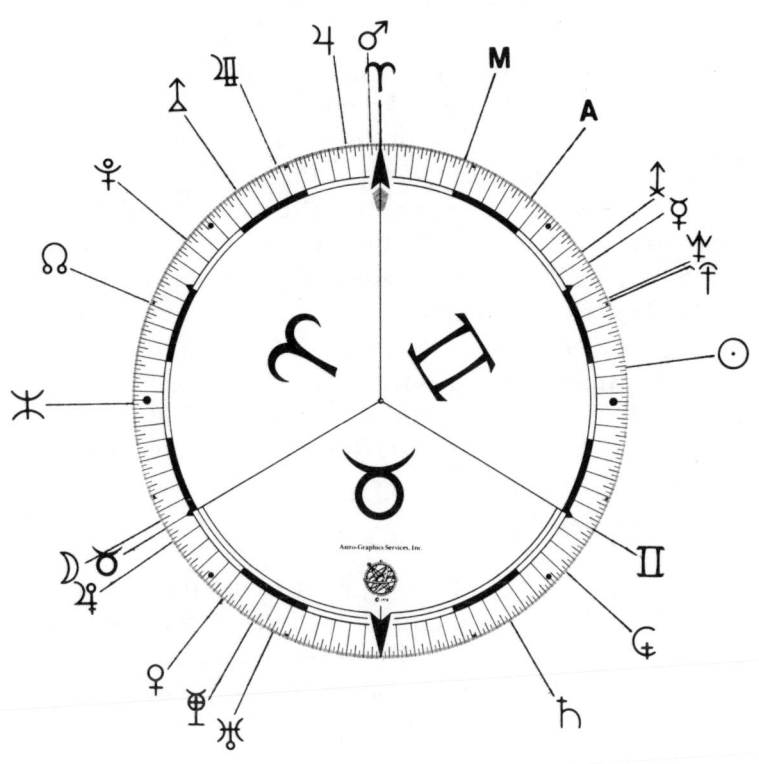

	Longitude	Latitude	Right Ascension	Declination
N. Node	16°LI58′	0°N00′	195° 38′	6°S40′
Cupido	0°SC58′	1°N03′	209° 13′	10°S49′
Hades	27°TA09′ ℞	1°S01′	55° 07′	18°N32′
Zeus	16°VI24′	0°N00′	167° 29′	5°N22′
Kronos	13°GE13′	0°N00′	71° 48′	22°N23′
Apollon	6°LI12′	0°N00′	185° 42′	2°S28′
Admetos	7°TA21′ ℞	0°N00′	34° 59′	13°N58′
Vulcanus	8°CN49′	0°N00′	99° 35′	23°N09′
Poseidon	22°LI40′	0°N00′	200° 58′	8°S49′
Ascendant	20°PI38′	0°N00′	351° 24′	3°S43′
Midheaven	25°SG01′	0°N00′	264° 34′	23°S21′

was anything consistently emphasized in this data and if there were correspondences in any way with the three starting point charts, my friend's chart, his brother's chart, or their composite. The major problem here was that certain degree areas of the natal charts were prominent in the departure charts, such as the degree of the natal Sun and the degree of the Midheaven of the plane departure trip, and it was difficult to determine which chart was activated at the time of an event. It must be made clear that this is not a legitimate scientific study because the subjective factors of Dennis' diary and my interpretation are too prominent, but it is the only way to proceed if one hopes to find anything at all in this data. There is much in astrology that cannot be easily, and objectively, tested. My investigation led to the following observations.

1. The chart for the plane flight was ruled out as a major influencing factor because its Midheaven was at 28 degrees of Gemini and the Ascendant at 28 degrees of Virgo, degree areas that duplicate Dennis' Sun position at 29 degrees Gemini. All events on the trip referred to this chart revealed only contacts with its angles.

2. The chart of departure from home seemed to be important and it appears as example chart 1A. The Midheaven of this chart is at 25 degrees of Sagittarius and the Ascendant is at 20½ degrees of Pisces, their midpoint being about 7¾ degrees of Aquarius. Uranus in this trip chart is at 8½ degrees of Scorpio and Venus at about 5 degrees of Leo, both linked to the the Ascendant/Midheaven midpoint by hard aspect. Even worse, Admetos, hypothetical planet of standstill and hindrance, is located at about 7½ of Taurus completing the symmetry. For a more visual description of this structure see the 90 degree chart in which the

Midheaven and Ascendant appear to be opposite the positions of Venus, Admetos, and Uranus. Interestingly, the Midheaven for the time that I began to examine this particular case study was at 7½ degrees of Scorpio and the transiting Moon at the time was at 8 degrees of Aquarius.

Other supporting factors for chart 1A are that the two most important meetings with people on the trip occurred when first the Sun and then Mercury crossed the Descendant. This is complicated by the fact that the degree of this Descendant is square the degree of the Midheaven in the natal composite chart, but since the Descendant rules others, I tend to lean towards chart 1A because it expresses the proper symbolism. The most beautiful day of the trip coincided with the transit of Venus trine the Midheaven. Transits of the Moon to the angles of this chart frequently coincided with the recorded events.

3. The chart of arrival at Shannon airport, appearing as example chart 1B — the beginning of the actual Ireland experience, must be seen as the "trip within a trip". Eight of the 17 events noted showed the Ascendant or Midheaven of this chart to be affected by the transiting angles, Moon, Venus, or Mercury within very close orbs. Some of the events had only approximate times and the transiting angles could not be used for analysis.

4. The Midheaven of the time that the brothers arrived at their home was within a few degrees of the Ascendant for chart 1A. Finally, relocated angles for chart 1A did not appear to correlate very well with the 17 events.

Both brothers thought the trip to be a disaster and this

54 / The Timing of Events: Electional Astrology

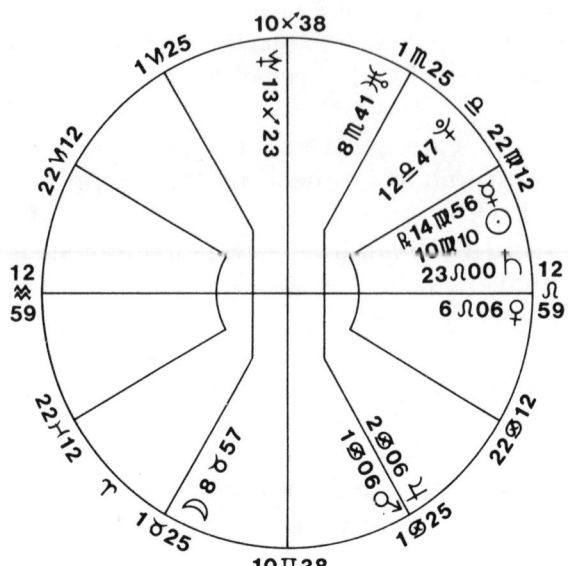

Chart 1 B

	Longitude	Latitude	Right Ascension	Declination
Sun	10°VI10′	0°N00′	161° 41′	7°N46′
Moon	8°TA57′	2°S04′	37° 14′	12°N32′
Mercury	14°VI56′ ℞	4°S13′	164° 29′	2°N02′
Venus	6°LE06′	0°S04′	128° 28′	18°N41′
Mars	1°CN06′	0°N04′	91° 12′	23°N30′
Jupiter	2°CN06′	0°S24′	92° 16′	23°N02′
Saturn	23°LE00′	1°N03′	145° 41′	14°N50′
Uranus	8°SC41′	0°N24′	216° 26′	14°S01′
Neptune	13°SG23′	1°N29′	252° 11′	20°S57′
Pluto	12°LI47′	16°N36′	198° 15′	10°N14′

Travel / 55

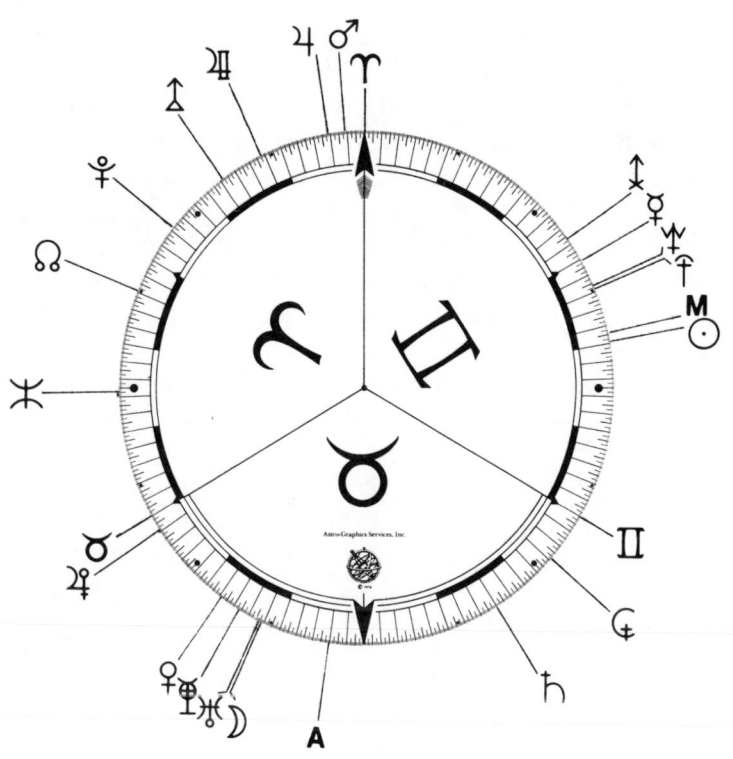

	Longitude	Latitude	Right Ascension	Declination
N. Node	16°LI55'	0°N00'	195° 36'	6°S39'
Cupido	0°SC59'	1°N03'	209° 14'	10°S50'
Hades	27°TA09' ℞	1°S01'	55° 07'	18°N32'
Zeus	16°VI25'	0°N00'	167° 30'	5°N22'
Kronos	13°GE13'	0°N00'	71° 48'	22°N23'
Apollon	6°LI13'	0°N00'	185° 42'	2°S28'
Admetos	7°TA20' ℞	0°N00'	34° 59'	13°N58'
Vulcanus	8°CN49'	0°N00'	99° 36'	23°N09'
Poseidon	22°LI40'	0°N00'	200° 58'	8°S49'
Ascendant	12°AQ59'	0°N00'	315° 27'	16°S55'
Midheaven	10°SG38'	0°N00'	249° 02'	22°S03'

was symbolized by the unfortunate symmetry of Uranus, Venus, and Admetos with the angles in chart 1A, only to be reinforced by the position of the Moon in chart 1B. Other traditionally agreed upon negative factors appear in these two charts. In 1A, the Moon is void of course, the ruler of the Ascendant is in the ninth square to Mercury — significator of mobility and travel, and Mercury is retrograde. In chart 1B, the Moon is opposed by the ruler of the Ascendant, Saturn is angular, and Neptune is very close to the Midheaven. This Neptune is also square to Mercury and the Sun which are both angular.

The start of a trip is the time when you have completed all your preparations and walk out the door of your house and enter the new experience ahead of you. This is the moment when you are irreversibly committed to the journey. If you start another trip while on your trip, you have two charts, the first referring to the general conditions of your entire experience and the second referring to the "trip within a trip". Besides the example of the Ireland trip and other flight trips examined, my experiences with backpacking trips has pointed this out very clearly. For example, I recently left my home at an elected time, drove for several hours, parked the car, noted the time, and began walking into the forest with camera in hand. Several weeks later I received by mail my processed film and noted carefully the time that I opened the package. While the degree of the Midheaven and Ascendant at this time was exactly the same as the Midheaven and Ascendant of the hike, there was no strong relationship to the chart for the main trip itself. If you start your main trip under favorable conditions all else falls into place and you will naturally select the right, or at least a good, time to begin other events on that trip. It may also be advisable, if you are planning to fly, to scrutinize the arrival time of your flight. That time would seem to be more important than the takeoff time, but still within the context of the chart for the time that you left your home.

Chart 2 is the chart of a trip to Shenandoah National Park during which my car's engine failed on Skyline Drive. I had originally planned to begin this trip at a much earlier hour but my companion on the journey, Gary Christen, was late in arriving at my house by a mere five hours. We left rather hastily noting the time as we pulled out of my driveway. An engine valve broke about eight PM when the transiting Midheaven opposed Saturn forcing us to spend the night at that location in the 15 degree cold. The next day my friend Dave found us and towed us home, the entire experience being quite exciting, surprisingly comfortable, and not nearly as expensive as it could have been.

The negative feature of this chart that makes it a good case study is the conjunction of the Sun, Uranus, and Mars square the Ascendant from the ninth house. Uranus is very close to an exact square, its declination at the time being exactly parallel to my natal Ascendant. I was prepared for some rough events on this trip, and if we had left at my original elected time this conjunction would have probably symbolized the hard hiking that we planned to do. The position of Uranus square the Ascendant and its significance as ruler of the Ascendant gave it too much control over the whole event. Jupiter almost exactly conjunct the IC indicated that some good would prevail. We ate very well, socialized during our visit to the park, and then were rescued. Robeson says that in the chart of a journey the Ascendant rules the place of departure, the 7th house the destination, the 10th the journey there, and the 4th the journey home. This appears to work in most travel chart and particularly in this one where the return trip was a rescue in a blue van. Among many other interesting and significant configurations in this chart is Saturn, which rules the twelfth house, exactly bi-septile (2/7) the Midheaven —

The Timing of Events: Electional Astrology

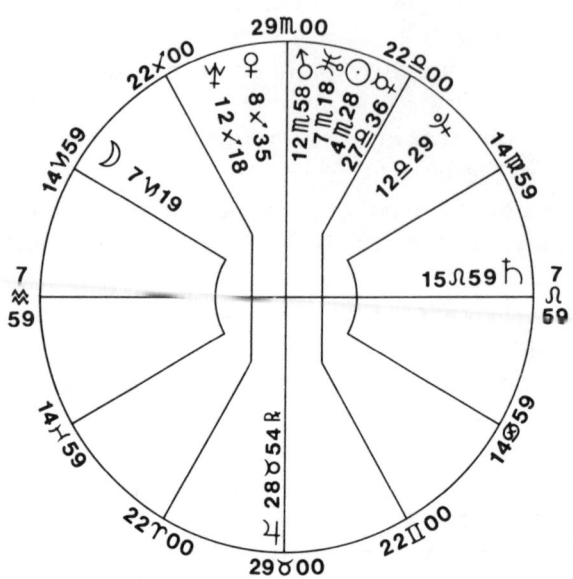

Chart 2

	Longitude	Latitude	Right Ascension	Declination
Sun	4°SC28'	0°N00'	212° 12'	13°S01'
Moon	7°CP19'	4°N46'	277° 42'	18°S29'
Mercury	27°LI36'	1°N16'	206° 05'	9°S26'
Venus	8°SG35'	1°S17'	246° 38'	23°S00'
Mars	12°SC58'	0°N01'	220° 31'	15°S43'
Jupiter	28°TA54' ℞	1°S09'	56° 56'	18°N47'
Saturn	15°LE59'	0°N41'	138° 40'	16°N42'
Uranus	7°SC18'	0°N26'	215° 05'	13°S32'
Neptune	12°SG18'	1°N28'	251° 02'	20°S49'
Pluto	12°LI29'	16°N29'	197° 56'	10°N15'

Travel / 59

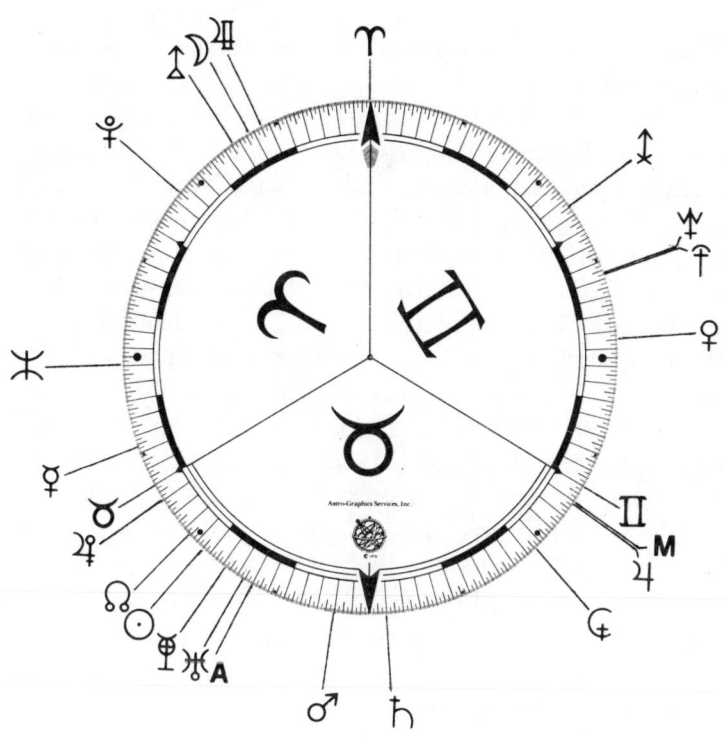

	Longitude	Latitude	Right Ascension	Declination
N. Node	3°SC20'	0°N00'	211° 07'	12°S38'
Cupido	0°SC59'	1°N03'	209° 13'	10°S51'
Hades	25°TA35' ℞	1°S01'	53° 31'	18°N10'
Zeus	16°VI33'	0°N00'	167° 37'	5°N19'
Kronos	12°GE16' ℞	0°N00'	70° 47'	22°N16'
Apollon	6°LI26'	0°N00'	185° 54'	2°S33'
Admetos	6°TA12' ℞	0°N00'	33° 53'	13°N35'
Vulcanus	8°CN22' ℞	0°N00'	99° 06'	23°N11'
Poseidon	22°LI52'	0°N00'	201° 09'	8°S53'
Ascendant	7°AQ59'	0°N00'	310° 24'	18°S16'
Midheaven	29°SC00'	0°N00'	236° 47'	19°S56'

an aspect suggesting serious limitations regarding objectives.

Chart 3 is an electional departure of one of the most perfect trips I have ever taken. I had the unique opportunity to place both the Sun and Jupiter almost exactly on the angles, the Sun ruling the 9th house and Jupiter ruling the Ascendant. My natal chart was "ripe" for travel during the weeks surrounding this trip and I took advantage of this condition by traveling frequently at this time. This trip to White Mountains National Forest was the culmination of this period. Transiting Jupiter was stationary at the antiscion of my natal Sun at the time and placing this extremely favorable (for myself) Jupiter on an angle brought out its potential for good fortune. Notice also that this Jupiter widely trines the 10th house planets. On a more subtle level, Jupiter is quintile Saturn in the 9th and the Sun, dominating the chart at the Midheaven, is at the midpoint between Jupiter and the cardinal points. An election like this is hard to arrive at. The weather on this trip was unusually perfect during the days that we were there and it began raining as we left the area. Photographic opportunities were in abundance and our timing (the coincidence factor) was nothing short of amazing.

Of all the backpacking trips that I have taken, the one that has left the greatest personal impact on me was one that had an Ascendant exactly (within 7 minutes of arc) opposite the Sun in my natal chart and the Midheaven within two degrees of a square to my natal Ascendant. This trip was a tough, gruelling hike in rapidly changing weather conditions in a very remote area, but I loved it. This brings up an important point to consider, that a person may not always want easy conditions in an event, but just the assurance that no really serious problems will develop. Placing Jupiter on an angle will usually cover this requirement, but to be an important and memorable event the election should also relate closely to the personal points in the natal chart.

Another point to consider is illustrated by the chart of a trip my wife and I took several years ago, an auto tour of Quebec and New England. The Midheaven of the trip was exactly square my natal Saturn and I tried to control the major choices as they arose. Needless to say, I made all the wrong decisions. If I had followed my wife's suggestions, (her natal Saturn was sextile the Sun and ruler of the Ascendant in the travel chart) we would have hit the weather patterns perfectly and had clear weather for the entire trip. As it was, I had us drive into a storm and then follow it on its slow trip east. Since that time I have always been sensitive to who is making the immediate decisions on a trip and the relation of their natal Saturn to the chart of the trip. Judging this factor is sometimes difficult, but as a general rule avoid, or be very cautious about, dominating decision making if your natal Saturn squares or opposes a prominent body or one of the angles in the chart of the trip.

A composite chart made from the chart of a trip and the natal chart of a person on that trip appears to show the nature of that person's experience of the trip. For example, a companion on a camping trip became very ill and was forced to stay in the tent for three days while I walked alone, with much pleasure, in the mountains. The composite of his birth chart and that of the trip had the Sun and Venus in Sagittarius square to Saturn, Uranus, and Pluto in Virgo. The composite of my birth chart and that of the trip had a massive conjunction of Saturn, Mercury, Uranus, Venus, Pluto, and the Sun in Virgo in the 12th house, but not squared or opposed by anything. Both charts had Jupiter rising, which was at the Midheaven of the trip chart, and we both adapted to the situation satisfactorily.

62 / *The Timing of Events: Electional Astrology*

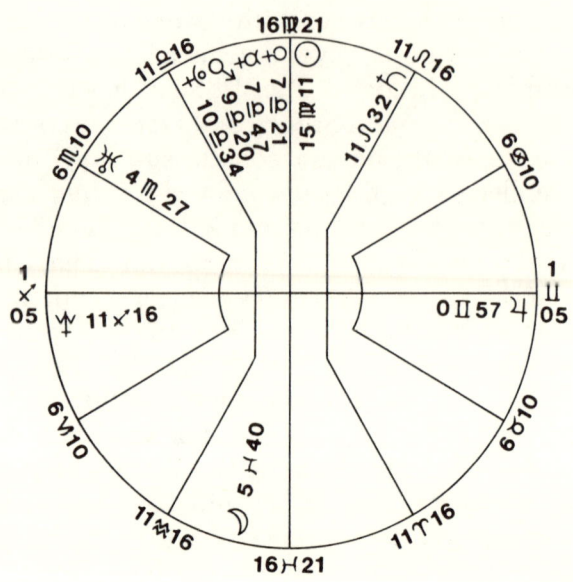

Chart 3

	Longitude	Latitude	Right Ascension	Declination
Sun	15°VI11'	0°N00'	166° 22'	5°N50'
Moon	5°PI40'	4°N23'	335° 51'	5°S21'
Mercury	7°LI47'	3°S55'	185° 36'	6°S41'
Venus	7°LI21'	0°N58'	187° 08'	2°S02'
Mars	9°LI20'	0°N31'	188° 47'	3°S14'
Jupiter	0°GE57'	1°S05'	59° 03'	19°N18'
Saturn	11°LE32'	0°N34'	134° 10'	17°N52'
Uranus	4°SC27'	0°N27'	212° 21'	12°S35'
Neptune	11°SG16'	1°N30'	249° 56'	20°S38'
Pluto	10°LI34'	16°N29'	196° 13'	10°N58'

Travel / 63

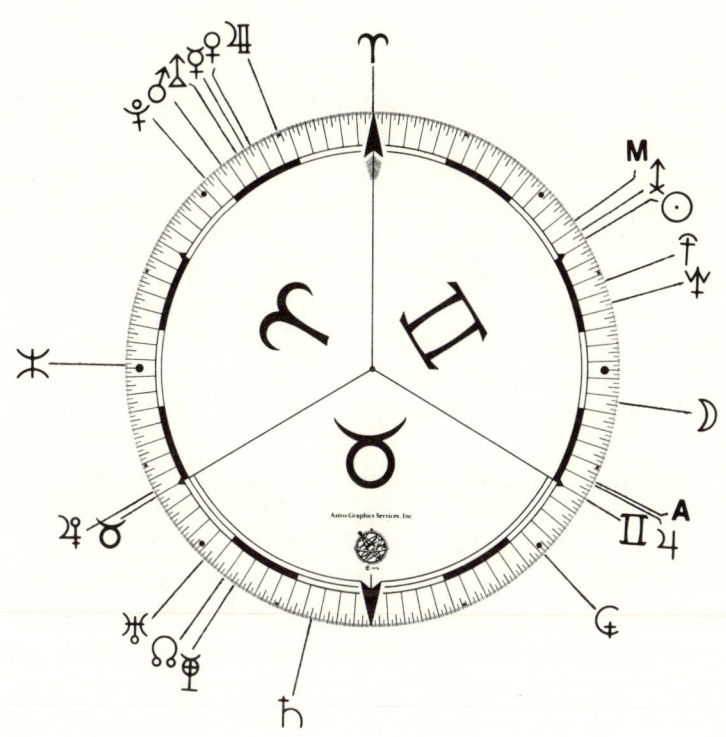

	Longitude	Latitude	Right Ascension	Declination
N. Node	5°SC59'	0°N00'	213° 40'	13°S31'
Cupido	29°LI43'	1°N03'	208° 01'	10°S24'
Hades	26°TA07' ℞	1°S01'	54° 03'	18°N18'
Zeus	15°VI43'	0°N00'	166° 51'	5°N38'
Kronos	12°GE32'	0°N00'	71° 04'	22°N18'
Apollon	5°LI40'	0°N00'	185° 12'	2°S15'
Admetos	6°TA43' ℞	0°N00'	34° 23'	13°N46'
Vulcanus	8°CN19'	0°N00'	99° 03'	23°N11'
Poseidon	22°LI15'	0°N00'	200° 34'	8°S40'
Ascendant	1°SG05'	0°N00'	238° 57'	20°S23'
Midheaven	16°VI21'	0°N00'	167° 27'	5°N23'

The Houses in Travel Charts

The first, third, and ninth houses are generally the most sensitive in travel charts and care should be taken, if electing a time, to keep them relatively free from affliction. The Ascendant will often describe the basic themes of the trip, or at least the nature of some of the more prominent events. For example, such things as a snake skin, a vulture, and the digging of a new hole for an outhouse were major features on a three day camping trip which had Scorpio rising. On a trip with Capricorn rising, a very old person was encountered along with many government workers.

The third and ninth houses seem to work similarly, a planet in one symbolizes nearly the same things as it would in the other. For example, Saturn in the third or ninth often symbolizes a long drive. Other points worth noting are that 29 degrees on an angle, or a prominent void of course Moon, will often symbolize confusion and uncertainty, and in many cases the need to change plans or backtrack. If no planets are in a house, often the planet in conjunction or in closest aspect with the ruler of the house will describe the situation adequately. As with all kinds of astrology, an emphasis of a particular sign will bend things toward the matters it symbolizes.

First house: The starting place, the general nature of the experience, the type of trip, dominant influences. The Moon here could mean changing conditions or perhaps a dominant woman. Pluto or Mars could mean a struggle over control of the trip.

Second house: The resources, money to spend and belongings brought along. Uranus here could suggest experimenting with resources, the use of gadgets, or even the sudden realization that something has been forgotten.

Third house: The conditions of transport. Pluto here could mean a shared ride, perhaps with a hitchhiker. Neptune suggests confusion and wrong turns.

Fourth house: The return journey, the weather conditions, the lodging conditions. Jupiter here means protection and generosity in connection with accomodations. In regard to the weather, the Sun or Mars often indicates hot weather, Saturn cold, Jupiter temperate, Uranus and Mercury are clear and windy, and the Moon, Venus, and Neptune indicate clouds, humidity, and rain.

Fifth house: Pleasurable activities, sport, entertainment. The Moon here can indicate eating pleasures, Neptune pleasures associated with water and institutions such as aquariums, zoos and museums.

Sixth house: Necessary adjustments, problems in travel, changes of schedule. Frequent adjustments would be indicated by the Moon. Neptune could mean not knowing what to do next.

Seventh house: The destination and persons encountered there. Mars here may indicate competition or friction at the destination, which may be appropriate depending on the purpose of the trip. Saturn could mean limited views (vistas) or constraints and laws to obey.

Eighth house: Shared expenses and food, communal supplies. Saturn here could mean resistance to sharing.

Ninth house: The experience of travel, the distance covered. A new experience would be symbolized by Uranus and a solo or pioneering experience by Mars.

Tenth house: The journey there, the purpose and objectives of the trip. Saturn in this house suggests a business trip, involvement with parents or officials, or simply a serious trip. Jupiter may mean that the trip is a learning experience while Uranus might symbolize a unique and different trip.

Eleventh house: The social conditions, groups of people encountered, and the pleasures of the trip. Mars here could mean marred pleasures through fighting, or positively, an exciting event. Saturn could mean disappointed expectations, older company, and delayed pleasures.

Twelfth house: Personal regrets and errors, confinements on the trip, experiences with institutions. Visits to art museums could be indicated by Venus, aquariums by Neptune.

Appropriate Planetary Pictures

When fine tuning an electional chart for a journey, the following typical planetary pictures (symmetrical groupings clearly visible on the 90 degree chart and dial) are suggested. Often variations are possible. If one or more of these combinations can be arranged in an election which also meets most of the traditional requirements (as seen in the traditional 12 house chart) the chances for success are tremendously enhanced.

Jupiter, Apollon, Sun = Midheaven/Mercury
(This means Jupiter, Apollon or Sun is at the midpoint of Midheaven and Mercury)

Mercury, Sun, Node = Midheaven/Jupiter

Mercury, Sun, Midheaven = Jupiter/Aries

Jupiter = Sun/Mercury

Mercury, Midheaven = Sun/Jupiter

Midheaven, Ascendant, Sun, Aries = Mercury/Jupiter

CHAPTER 5

Weddings

There is already considerable information available on the selection of a favorable day and time for a marriage, most of it found in the sources already mentioned. There is no doubt that the chart for the exact time of a wedding is significant; case studies have pointed this out very clearly. A major problem is in regard to the exact location of the significant moment within the marriage ceremony. The actual marriage ritual is often very short, under ten minutes, which in most elections would not create major changes in the chart. But the question still remains; should the chart be cast for the beginning of the ceremony, the exchange of rings, the vows, or the official pronouncement of man and wife? The latter is certainly the irrevocable part of the ceremony, but it is also possible that the symbolic ring ritual may be its focal point. In many of the case studies available to me I have only approximate times for the ceremony, within five minutes or so, which is not specific enough to resolve this problem. It is hard to find a religious official that will regulate his ceremony for the sake of astrology, and in the weddings that I have elected, I merely indicate that the ceremony should start shortly before the elected time. Due to the private nature of a marriage, I have had few opportunities to examine in detail the wedding charts that I have elected, with the exception of event correlations such as births and residence changes. At the present time I favor the official pronouncement as the critical moment.

The object in the election of a time for a wedding is not

Weddings / 69

to reach perfection (which is usually impossible unless the natal charts of the partners are extremely harmonious) but to adjust circumstances by emphasizing the desirable and de-emphasizing the undesirable. When narrowing the field of possibilities through the use of directions and progressions, look for the following contacts which appropriately symbolize the event. For males, the Midheaven, Ascendant, or Sun should be progressed or directed to Venus, the Moon, or the ruler of the 7th house. For females the Moon, Midheaven, and Ascendant should be linked by progression or direction with the Sun, Mars, Venus, or the ruler of the 7th. It is important to note that a prominent Saturn at the time of the wedding, prominent due to transits, progressions, or directions, is not necessarily an unfavorable omen. Certainly an afflicted and debilitated Saturn may signify serious problems which may be unavoidable if the marriage is, in the (non-astrological) eyes of a good judge of these matters, an unfortunate event. A good Saturn, on the other hand, can signify an enduring event and one in which traditions and parents play an important part. Due to the fact that a marriage ceremony is a ritual and a formal event, I am inclined to seek out in such an election a good, well placed Saturn.

Convenience and custom are usually of such importance in the planning of a wedding date that the astrologer becomes severely handicapped in his work. When constrained by date limitations, put Venus and Jupiter on an angle or make them prominent in some way. Symmetry including Venus, Jupiter, Cupido and the angles is another way of obtaining relatively favorable circumstances in a wedding. It should be noted that planetary pictures have the most power in the chart when the planets and angles involved are in some aspect with each other (including the minor aspects) or are in aspect to major points in the natal charts or in the composite. Remember that if the election does not relate to the person or persons experiencing it, it will tend to have less meaning in their lives. A good approach would be to have transiting Venus aspecting both persons charts in some way, and on that day have the wedding occur when Venus was culminating. Very often couples have shared areas or degrees of the zodiac which can be used in this way, provided there are no negative natal implications. In a wedding chart the Moon, Venus, and the Ascendant are probably the most important factors and they should not be seriously afflicted and prominent at the same time.

The first and seventh houses of the wedding chart are of particular importance and a favorable aspect between their rulers is desirable. The ruler of the first house should also be well aspected, preferably in conjunction or good aspect to Venus, the Sun, or Jupiter. Traditionally it is said that the Ascendant, its ruler, and the Sun symbolize the husband while the Descendant, its ruler, and Venus symbolize the wife. This may actually be just a reflection of socio-cultural traditions, as is much of traditional astrology. Perhaps the Ascendant symbolizes the dominant partner. The tenth house rules the events and fortunes following marriage and the fourth house rules the home and the final outcome of the event. Mercury and the fifth house indicate children, and if Mercury is strong in the chart and placed in a water sign, it is said that children will soon follow. Afflictions in a wedding chart will indicate the problem areas. Other traditional considerations can be found in the sources on electional astrology mentioned earlier.

Unlike charts for journeys, wedding charts symbolize just one aspect of a multifaceted situation. In a partnership several charts are relevant including one for the first meeting, the time/space relationship chart, and the composite chart. In electing a chart for a wedding, the nature of these other charts should be considered and hopefully improved upon. For example, if the composite chart showed financial problems, the second house in the wedding chart could be purposely enhanced to modify this pattern. This is probably the place to mention the fact that a couple not suited for marriage to each other will probably not be able to find a good electional time for a marriage ceremony. Astrology mirrors reality.

The Houses in Wedding Charts

1. The general situation, the main themes and overall tone.

2. Resources, financial matters, income, possessions.

3. Environmental contacts, transportation, relatives, neighbors.

4. The home, property, the families and parents, inner bonding.

5. Children, pleasurable activities.

6. Sickness, problems in adjustments, schedule conflicts.

7. Co-operation, the issue of partnership.

8. Sharing, sexuality, divorce, borrowed money, inheritance, investments.

9. Broadening experiences, travel, awareness, education, legal matters.

10. The sense of direction and purpose, public image.

11. Friends and group associations, expectations.

72 / The Timing of Events: Electional Astrology

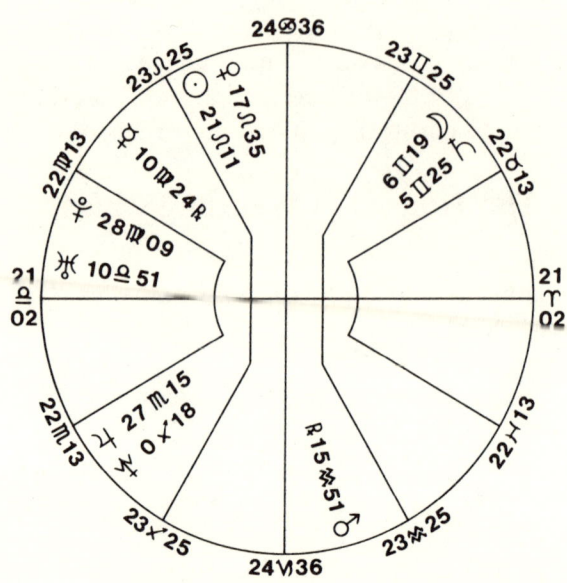

Chart 4

	Longitude	Latitude	Right Ascension	Declination
Sun	21°LE11'	0°N00'	143° 34'	14°N26'
Moon	6°GE19'	4°N55'	63° 30'	26°N12'
Mercury	10°VI24' ℞	4°S12'	160° 19'	3°N46'
Venus	17°LE35'	1°N10'	140° 24'	16°N41'
Mars	15°AQ51' ℞	6°S50'	320° 30'	22°S36'
Jupiter	27°SC15'	0°N43'	235° 09'	18°S51'
Saturn	5°GE25'	1°S58'	63° 52'	19°N16'
Uranus	10°LI51'	0°N39'	190° 14'	3°S42'
Neptune	0°SG18'	1°N40'	238° 30'	18°S35'
Pluto	28°VI09'	15°N42'	184° 42'	15°N07'

Weddings / 73

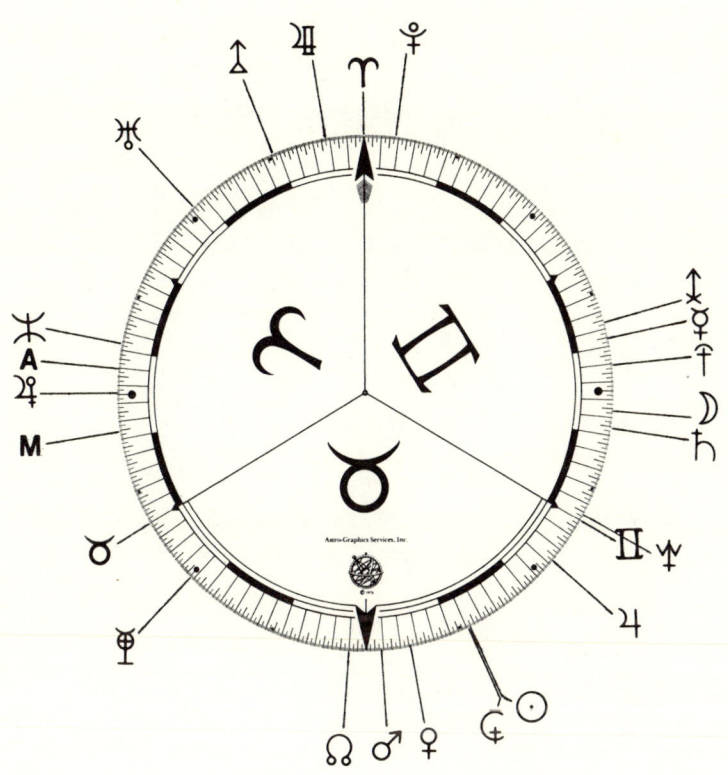

	Longitude	Latitude	Right Ascension	Declination
N. Node	14°AQ01′	0°N00′	316° 29′	16°S38′
Cupido	22°LI27′	1°N01′	201° 09′	7°S47′
Hades	21°TA04′	0°S58′	48° 54′	17°N05′
Zeus	11°VI19′	0°N00′	162° 46′	7°N19′
Kronos	8°GE56′	0°N00′	67° 14′	21°N48′
Apollon	2°LI15′	0°N00′	182° 04′	0°S54′
Admetos	3°TA54′ ℞	0°N00′	31° 39′	12°N49′
Vulcanus	5°CN24′	0°N00′	95° 53′	23°N20′
Poseidon	19°LI37′	0°N00′	198° 06′	7°S40′
Ascendant	21°LI02′	0°N00′	199° 26′	8°S12′
Midheaven	24°CN36′	0°N00′	116° 31′	21°N12′

12. Errors, separations relating to confinement, critical adjustments, unconscious behaviors, hospitalization.

Appropriate Planetary Pictures

Assuming the basic traditional requirements for an election have been met, the following planetary pictures (visible in 90 degree format) are suggested. Try to include at least one of the following (or a similar variation) for best results in electing a time for a wedding ceremony.

Cupido or Venus = Midheaven/Sun or Midheaven/Jupiter

Ascendant, Venus or Jupiter = Midheaven/Cupido or Sun/Cupido

Sun, Jupiter or Cupido = Midheaven/Venus

Ascendant, Mercury, Jupiter or Midheaven = Sun/Venus

Ascendant, Node, Venus or Jupiter = Sun/Moon

Mercury, Venus, Cupido or Midheaven = Moon/Jupiter

Ascendant, Mercury, Cupido, Jupiter or Midheaven = Venus/Node or Venus/Aries

Case Studies

In the first example, chart 4, the couple married impulsively and their marriage lasted only a few months. Their separation was permanent and they never saw each other again. I was on hand for the wedding, which

Weddings / 75

took place in the bride's backyard, and noted that the main part of the ceremony was centered around 11:15 AM.

An examination of the natal charts at the time of the wedding shows clearly that from progressions and transits alone there were serious problems. In the husband's chart a conjunction of the progressed Sun and Venus was occurring at the midpoint of an exact Mars-Neptune sextile in the natal chart. This could be interpreted as indicating distorted expectations about love complicated by strong sexual drives. Pluto was transiting by conjunction his natal Saturn (difficult transformation) and Saturn was sesquiquadrate (3/8) his natal Venus. This is scarcely a happy combination. I should also mention that transiting Jupiter was forming a square to his natal Jupiter which rules the cusp of his seventh house, Sagittarius. The bride's chart had even worse indicators. Her progressed Mars, ruler of her seventh house, was within one degree of opposition to her Ascendant. Her progressed Sun was exactly in conjunction with her natal Mars, natally opposed by Saturn and square Uranus. At the time of the wedding transiting Pluto was in opposition to this natal Mars. This woman was headstrong.

The chart for the wedding clearly reflected this potential disaster. The Moon is conjunct Saturn in the 8th house and this conjunction is opposite Neptune and square to Mercury. The Moon-Saturn conjunction is at the midpoint of this somewhat wide Neptune-Mercury square bringing its power for chaos into focus. Worse yet, this Moon-Saturn conjunction is sesquiquadrate (3/8) the Ascendant. The Moon and the Ascendant, major points of concern in any election, are linked with Saturn, which in turn is linked to a Mercury-Neptune square. Dishonesty and cooled feelings are suggested very clearly. This combination can be seen rather easily on the 90 degree dial. Also suggested here is that the marriage would have

The Timing of Events: Electional Astrology

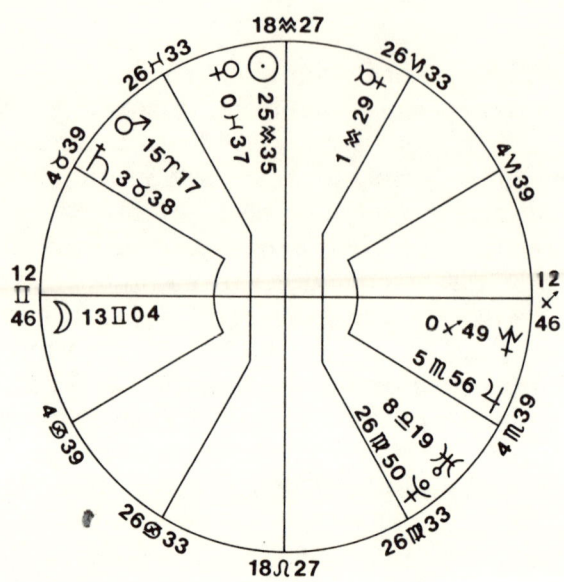

Chart 5

	Longitude	Latitude	Right Ascension	Declination
Sun	25°AQ35'	0°N00'	327° 51'	13°S00'
Moon	13°GE04'	5°N16'	70° 54'	27°N36'
Mercury	1°AQ29'	0°S38'	303° 52'	20°S27'
Venus	0°PI37'	1°S26'	333° 12'	12°S36'
Mars	15°AR17'	0°S05'	14° 06'	5°N57'
Jupiter	5°SC56'	1°N21'	214° 05'	12°S13'
Saturn	3°TA38'	2°S19'	32° 12'	10°N33'
Uranus	8°LI19' ℞	0°N45'	187° 56'	2°S37'
Neptune	0°SG49'	1°N41'	239° 02'	18°S40'
Pluto	26°VI50' ℞	16°N09'	183° 42'	16°N03'

Weddings / 77

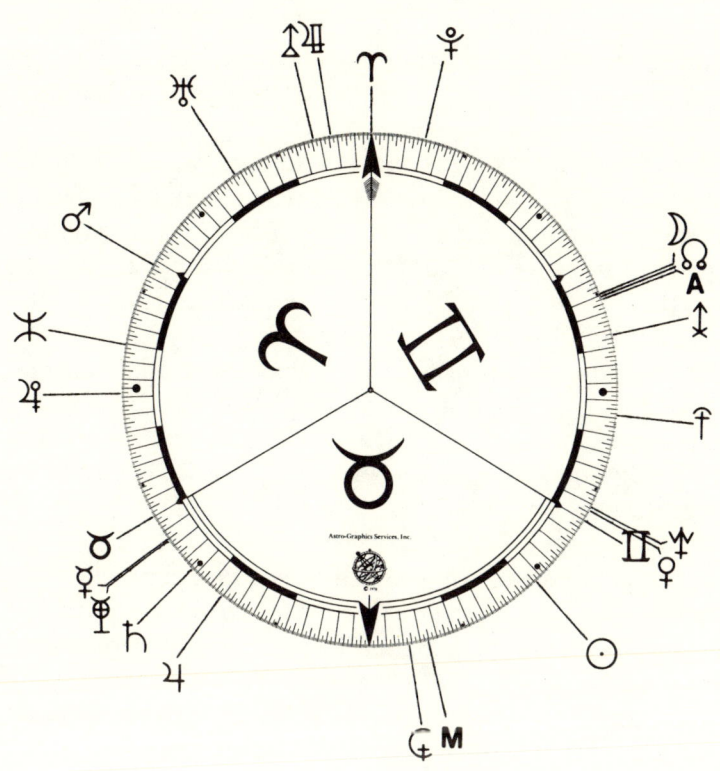

	Longitude	Latitude	Right Ascension	Declination
N. Node	12°PI55'	0°N00'	344° 15'	6°S43'
Cupido	22°LI47' ℞	1°N02'	201° 28'	7°S54'
Hades	17°TA18'	0°S57'	45° 07'	16°N05'
Zeus	10°VI42' ℞	0°N00'	162° 12'	7°N33'
Kronos	6°GE11' ℞	0°N00'	64° 19'	21°N21'
Apollon	2°LI21' ℞	0°N00'	182° 09'	0°S56'
Admetos	1°TA34'	0°N00'	29° 25'	12°N01'
Vulcanus	3°CN29' ℞	0°N00'	93° 47'	23°N24'
Poseidon	20°LI02' ℞	0°N00'	198° 30'	7°S50'
Ascendant	12°GE46'	0°N00'	71° 19'	22°N20'
Midheaven	18°AQ27'	0°N00'	320° 53'	15°S18'

great difficulties renewing itself possibly due to blockages of a sexual nature (8th house). The very close Sun-Hades square is a further indicator of an unpleasant situation.

Also prominent in this chart is the Sun-Venus conjunction in the 10th house opposed by Mars in the 4th. This is very significant because not only are Mars and Venus basic significators of love and attraction, but they are also the rulers of the 7th and 1st houses and are emphasized by their angularity. Their linkage to the Sun, the third personal point afflicted in this chart, also emphasizes the great tensions, sexual and otherwise, in this marriage. One final note, the traditional via combusta, or 15 degrees Libra to 15 degrees Scorpio contains the Ascendant.

A second example of a wedding is chart 5, an election. The electional process in this case was quite difficult as I had a narrow range in which to select a favorable time. The final decision turned out to be Valentine's day, which drew no complaints from either family as that day fell on a weekend in that year. My objectives were basically to put anything difficult in the background and anything good up front, thus insuring a good reputation for the event. At the time, Saturn was transiting by square the bride's Jupiter and the husband's Mars which natally oppose each other. In order to supposedly minimize this transit I arranged to have Saturn near the 12th house and not angular. Unfortunately this Saturn squares Mercury, ruler of the chart, but a Mercury square Saturn from the 12th to the 9th is more desirable than having this square right on the angles which would have occurred at several other times that day. Also notice that Venus is square Neptune in this wedding. It is desirable to have Venus prominent in a wedding chart but the square to Neptune is suspect, to say the least. However, both these people have Libra rising and Neptune nearby natally and they should be familiar with this Neptunian vibration. My strategy was to accent Venus and strengthen it by placing it in the 10th house conjunct the Sun. Besides receiving the direct energies of the Sun, Venus is also semisextile Mercury (ruler of first) which is sextile Neptune, thus any potential Venus-Neptune problems are communicated and cleared up mentally.

The Sun and Moon are the dominant bodies in this chart and give it power due to their angularity. Both luminaries form favorable aspects to the natal charts and are relatively unafflicted. I think that these factors have most accurately signified the nature of the marriage. The honorable status of the marriage with Aquarian overtones (astrological timing and Unitarian ceremony) relates to the position of the Sun. Note also that the Sun stands at the midpoint of Midheaven/Venus and Moon/Jupiter as seen on the 90 degree chart. Also, Jupiter is located at the midpoint of Midheaven/Cupido. The strong domestic urge to own, remodel, and decorate their home is indicated by the Moon conjunct the Ascendant and square its node. Normally it is not a good idea to place the Moon in such a prominent and potentially vulnerable position, but Gemini isn't quite like the water signs, and with elections you can't always get what you want. This Moon is trine the man's Sun and conjunct the woman's Mercury.

This couple bought their home when a Sun-Uranus conjunction fell exactly trine to the wedding chart's rising Moon and when Mars was transiting the Midheaven. The birth of a boy occurred when transiting Jupiter trined the chart's Mercury, generally said to rule the children of the marriage, but in this case also ruler of the fifth house. A second child was born when Jupiter opposed this Mercury. One final note on this chart. I elected this time well before I had ever heard of composite charts but the basic similarity of the composite to the elected

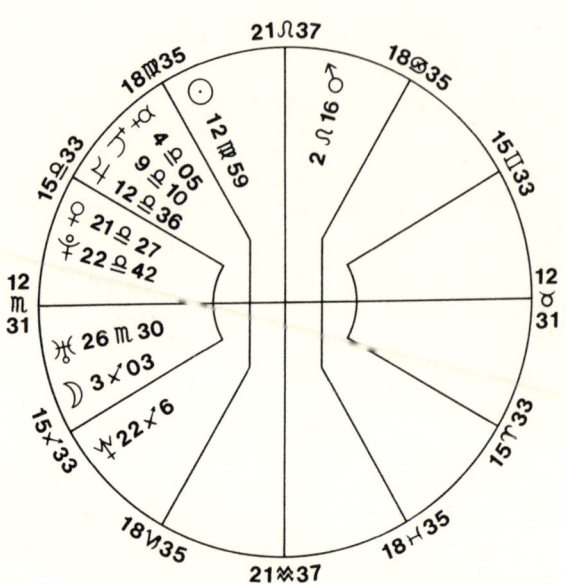

Chart 6

	Longitude	Latitude	Right Ascension	Declination
Sun	12°VI59'	0°N00'	164° 19'	6°N41'
Moon	3°SG03'	4°N22'	241° 54'	16°S29'
Mercury	4°LI05'	0°S23'	183° 36'	1°S58'
Venus	21°LI27'	0°S10'	199° 45'	8°S31'
Mars	2°LE16'	1°N00'	124° 47'	20°N37'
Jupiter	12°LI36'	1°N07'	192° 02'	3°S57'
Saturn	9°LI10'	2°N14'	189° 18'	1°S35'
Uranus	26°SC30'	0°N11'	234° 14'	19°S11'
Neptune	22°SG06'	1°N19'	261° 29'	21°S54'
Pluto	22°LI42'	16°N41'	207° 09'	6°N40'

Weddings / 81

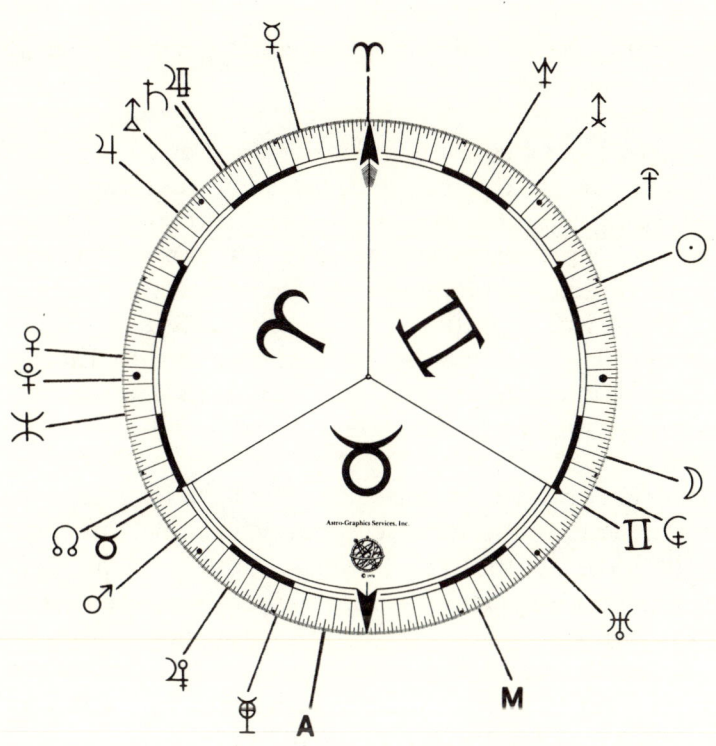

	Longitude	Latitude	Right Ascension	Declination
N. Node	29°CN24′	0°N00′	121° 34′	20°N17′
Cupido	6°SC30′	1°N04′	214° 32′	12°S41′
Hades	1°GE13′ ℞	1°S02′	59° 18′	19°N24′
Zeus	19°VI37′	0°N00′	170° 28′	4°N07′
Kronos	16°GE02′	0°N00′	74° 50′	22°N43′
Apollon	8°LI43′	0°N00′	188° 01′	3°S28′
Admetos	9°TA40′ ℞	0°N00′	37° 16′	14°N43′
Vulcanus	11°CN00′	0°N00′	101° 58′	22°N59′
Poseidon	24°LI37′	0°N00′	202° 48′	9°S32′
Ascendant	12°SC31′	0°N00′	220° 04′	15°S36′
Midheaven	21°LE37′	0°N00′	143° 59′	14°N18′

wedding chart is rather amazing. The most obvious factors in common are a Sun-Venus conjunction in the 10th house and a Saturn-Mercury linkage, in the composite it is by conjunction.

Chart 6 is an election which was not used for a wedding. The couple did get married soon afterward, but because of religious objections, had turned down my offer to set a precise time. The day itself, a Saturday, was a good choice astrologically for the following reasons. The Moon was unafflicted and applying to a sextile to Mercury. The Sun was in close semisextile to Jupiter and Venus was moving towards a sextile to Neptune and a conjunction to an unafflicted Pluto.

The chart presented here is a chart for a time 20 minutes earlier than the actual ceremony. I believe this chart would have symbolized a more stable and positive moment in time. The Ascendant here is positioned so that it is in very close sextile to the Sun and semisextile to Jupiter. In terms of planetary symmetry, this means Jupiter is at the Sun/Ascendant midpoint, a symbol of good luck and joint success. Venus is positioned almost exactly sextile to the Midheaven and both Pluto and Neptune favorably aspect this Midheaven. The Moon, though in the first house, is applying to a sextile to Mercury and a septile to Jupiter. Clearly, the morning was a good time of day to have a wedding, an afternoon wedding on this date would have the Moon in applying square to the Sun.

This example further illustrates the detailed use of planetary symmetry in the fine tuning of an election. Planetary pictures involving the Ascendant and the Midheaven change dramatically every few minutes and it is advisable to screen such patterns carefully before an elected time is set. In this chart we have Jupiter positioned at the Moon/Midheaven midpoint, suggesting powerful and deep feelings about the world and success in establishing a home. As was mentioned already, Jupiter is also at the midpoint of the Sun and Ascendant. This chart gets a lot of mileage out of Jupiter. The Moon is square to the midpoint of the Midheaven and the Sun, suggesting a strong input of subconscious and instinctive directives in the matter. The Ascendant stands at the midpoint of the Moon and Venus, a particularly good picture for a wedding as this suggests that love and affection are prominent. The hypothetical planet Cupido, which is associated with marriages and other community and family affairs, is positioned by semisquare to the midpoint of Venus and the Midheaven.

All of the above symbolism is favorable and appropriate for a wedding but, unfortunately, in this case it was missed by a mere 20 minutes. The actual wedding ceremony took place as the Midheaven closed into a square with Uranus, ruler of the fourth house. The couple has had to move abruptly several times due to job opportunities. They also have mentioned their sense of social isolation as a result of these changes.

Chapter 6

Business and Employment

The use of astrology in the business world may eventually become commonplace. Businessmen are always looking for ways to increase efficiency (and profits) and willingly pay stiff professional fees for surveys and projections of future economic conditions. Although business astrology in the future will probably utilize graphic representations of planetary phenomena, there will still remain the need to refer back to the two most critical charts in any business enterprise, the chart of the official beginning of the business, and the chart of the person in charge. Both of these may be plural.

The official beginning of a business is in many instances a questionable point in time. Incorporation dates and times certainly work and should always be investigated. Opening day, opening bank account and paper signing charts are also valuable and are useful charts for a business even if they only refer to the opening of the books and financial records. The birth of a business is when it becomes both an operating entity in the world and a part of the legal structure. A large business would have an incorporation chart and a chart for the onset of the first business day. A small store would have opening day, its first public "appearance", as its most important chart. Whether the time of the first transaction, that first dollar on the wall, is more significant than the publicly announced time of opening, is a moot point.

Experience has indicated the following. Incorporation charts always hold some kind of background tone for a business. Any re-incorporations will have astrological significance if the re-incorporation resulted in reorganization and consequent divergence and separation from the past. While a re-incorporation usually does result in some legal, clerical and financial rearrangements, a re-incorporation chart is only as strong as the actual changes.

I have observed astrologically what appeared to be a struggle between an incorporation chart and a re-incoporation chart that was trying to assert its independence. The incorporation chart showed a series of crisis indicators mostly focused on Midheaven, Mars, and Admetos coming together by solar arc directions. This suggests a major standstill/stalemate related to management problems. At the same time the re-incorporation chart showed Mercury retrograde coming to the Sun and the Sun coming to Mercury simultaneously by secondary progressions. This event occured about three months after re-incorporation and suggested to me that the "ego consciousness" of the company was at a critical point. What was actually happening was that the management was being forced to deal with certain changes. They had made several structural changes at the time of re-incorporation but hadn't taken them seriously until severe market pressures forced them to be decisive. The re-incorporation was such that a branch of a large corporation became more of an independent office. Acceptance of this fact occurred only when the symbolism in both charts indicated that it would, or at least some kind of crisis would be precipitated. The original incorporation chart continued to be useful.

I have had the opportunity to record the formation point of several musical groups and observe their rise and fall. This information is presented because it can be applied to other situations in which a group of people come together for a particular purpose. I have found that the best working chart for a group is the time that all the members of the group assemble together for the first time and begin their business. The leader or focal point of the group, and there usually is one, must be present. I have also found that this beginning point does not seem to be altered significantly when members of the group leave or new persons join. If the leader leaves the group, then the situation becomes questionable, unless a democratic process has been in effect all along and changes in power have been prepared for. Ultimately, astrology reflects how life really is.

Charts made for trips or for weddings are charts that affect very few people. A business usually deals with the public and can be affected by the general economy. Because of this, attention to mundane factors is far more important when electing a chart for a business than it has been for our previous topics. In my experience, the two most important mundane considerations are:

1. The symmetry around the Aries point or other cardinal points in the electional chart.

2. The relationship of important components of the chart to the degrees of previous eclipses and planetary stations.

The Planets in the Houses of Business Charts

Sun: The Sun draws a focus on the issues of the house it is in. These issues should be faced squarely in order for the business to succeed.

Moon: The Moon tends to make matters ruled by its house somewhat unclear and even irrational. The house position of the Moon often symbolizes the weakest or most sensitive areas of the business.

Business and Employment / 87

Mercury: Mercury usually symbolizes the efficient functioning of the house that it is in, unless it is badly afflicted.

Venus: Venus is generally a good omen for those things ruled by its house, but often it does not give enough push or energy to make the kind of progress that would be desirable in a business.

Mars: This is one of the most important planets in a business chart as it accounts for initiative and competitiveness. It tends towards accomplishment if angular.

Jupiter: Jupiter nearly always has a positive influence on any house, unless it is heavily afflicted. It usually symbolizes a concern with travel or legal matters for those things ruled by the house it is in.

Saturn: Saturn presents problems, restrictions, and limitations often brought about by authority figures or even the government. Saturn in a house indicates that the matters ruled by the house should be very carefully organized.

Uranus: The matters of the house that Uranus is in tend to function erratically and often independently. It can also symbolize advanced techniques applied to these areas.

Neptune: Like the Moon, Neptune tends to confuse the matters ruled by its house. Often it suggests that some kind of ideology is directing things in those areas.

Pluto: Pluto's house position usually refers to the area of the business in which crisis conditions are most prevalent. There is often a struggle over the issues symbolized by its house placement. Sharing seems to be both the

88 / *The Timing of Events: Electional Astrology*

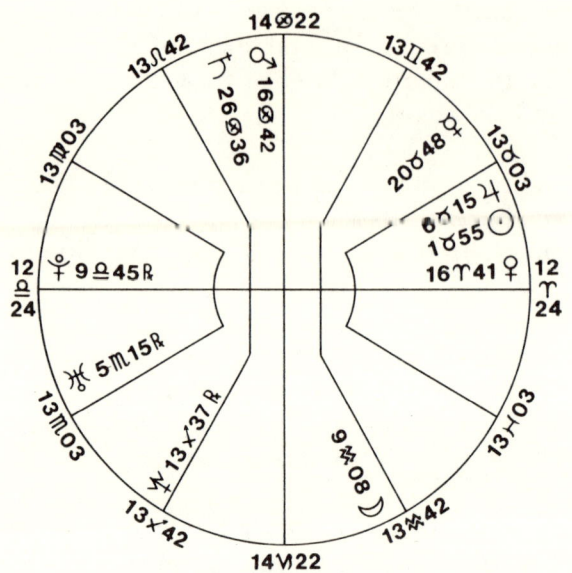

Chart 7

	Longitude	Latitude	Right Ascension	Declination
Sun	1°TA55′	0°N00′	29° 45′	12°N08′
Moon	9°AQ08′	5°N16′	310° 09′	12°S53′
Mercury	20°TA48′	2°N18′	47° 43′	20°N10′
Venus	16°AR41′	1°S29′	15° 57′	5°N12′
Mars	16°CN42′	1°N54′	108° 22′	24°N17′
Jupiter	6°TA15′	0°S58′	34° 15′	12°N41′
Saturn	26°CN36′	0°N24′	118° 42′	21°N14′
Uranus	5°SC15′ ℞	0°N31′	213° 08′	12°S47′
Neptune	13°SG37′ ℞	1°N34′	252° 26′	20°S53′
Pluto	9°LI45′ ℞	17°N27′	195° 52′	12°N10′

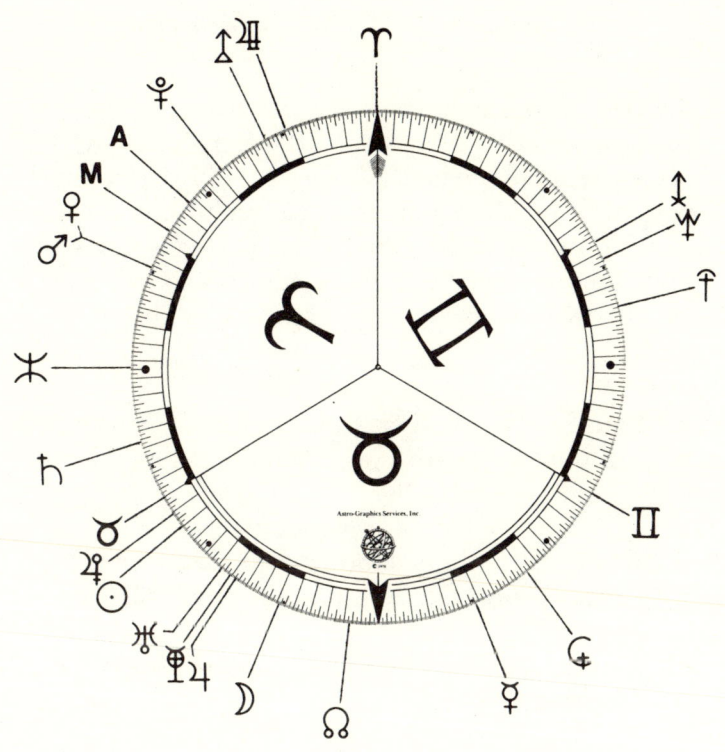

	Longitude	Latitude	Right Ascension	Declination
N. Node	13°SC20'	0°N00'	220° 53'	15°S51'
Cupido	0°SC09' ℞	1°N05'	208° 26'	10°S30'
Hades	24°TA14'	0°S59'	52° 07'	17°N53'
Zeus	14°VI42' ℞	0°N00'	165° 55'	6°N01'
Kronos	10°GE49'	0°N00'	69° 14'	22°N04'
Apollon	5°LI21' ℞	0°N00'	184° 55'	2°S08'
Admetos	5°TA50'	0°N00'	33° 31'	13°N28'
Vulcanus	6°CN45'	0°N00'	97° 21'	23°N16'
Poseidon	22°LI22' ℞	0°N00'	200° 41'	8°S42'
Ascendant	12°LI24'	0°N00'	191° 24'	4°S54'
Midheaven	14°CN22'	0°N00'	105° 36'	22°N40'

problem and the solution.

The Houses in Business Charts

First house: The business organization itself, the general situation and the attitude of the personnel. Rising planets are often the most descriptive in the entire chart. For example, Mars here makes for a forceful, competitive business. Jupiter here often indicates that travel or shipping may be prominent activities. Pluto can symbolize a change in ownership or deep changes in the general situation.

Second house: The budget, liquid assets, earning and purchasing power, persons who handle financial matters.

Third house: Telephone and communications, messages, transportation factors and departments.

Fourth house: The building (office) and property, real estate investments.

Fifth house: The development of resources, speculation, entertainment. The product of the business.

Sixth house: Employees, sickness, scheduling changes, labor unions.

Seventh house: Relations with the public and with other companies, mergers, agreements and competition.

Eighth house: Loans and debts, joint financial projects, losses or gains from deaths, inheritances.

Ninth house: Publishing, advertising, legal matters, travel, educational programs.

Tenth house: The boss or management, the announced objectives, reputation and status.

Eleventh house: Advisory groups, company policies, social activities, association memberships.

Twelfth house: Secret activities, plots, errors and misgivings, dealings with institutions, intelligence gathering.

Appropriate Planetary Pictures

After meeting the traditional basic requirements for a business election, including attention given to linkage with previous eclipses and stations, try to include at least one of the following for best results in electing a time for a business to begin operations or become incorporated.

Moon, Jupiter or Apollon = Midheaven/Aries, Midheaven/Sun or Midheaven/Ascendant

Sun, Apollon or Node = Jupiter/Aries or Jupiter/Midheaven

Midheaven, Sun or Aries = Jupiter/Pluto or Jupiter/Moon

Apollon, Midheaven or Aries = Sun/Jupiter

Sun, Jupiter or Apollon = Aries/Node

Case Studies

Chart 7 is that of the announced opening of a restaurant. The building itself was an 18th century farm house and much work had to be done to modernize it. The owner-builder was under constant harassment from his wife

92 / *The Timing of Events: Electional Astrology*

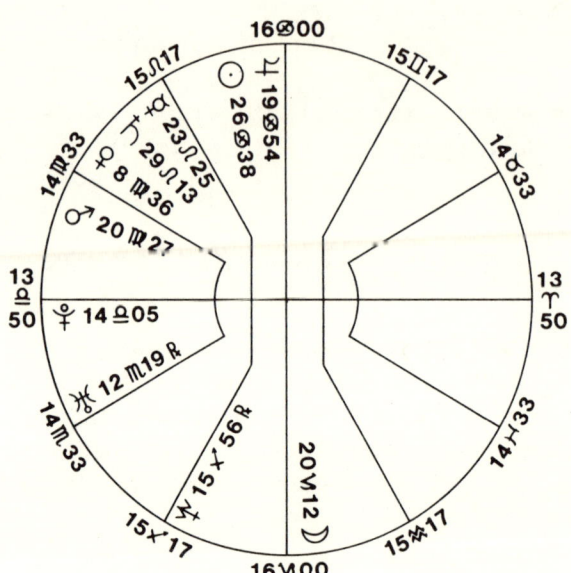

Chart 8

	Longitude	Latitude	Right Ascension	Declination
Sun	26°CN38'	0°N00'	118° 40'	20°N50'
Moon	20°CP12'	4°N43'	291° 07'	17°S16'
Mercury	23°LE25'	0°S27'	145° 36'	13°N17'
Venus	8°VI36'	1°N09'	160° 40'	9°N25'
Mars	20°VI27'	0°N43'	171° 31'	4°N26'
Jupiter	19°CN54'	0°N10'	111° 34'	22°N07'
Saturn	29°LE13'	1°N26'	151° 51'	13°N06'
Uranus	12°SC19' ℞	0°N23'	219° 59'	15°S11'
Neptune	15°SG56' ℞	1°N29'	254° 54'	21°S14'
Pluto	14°LI05'	16°N59'	199° 34'	10°N06'

Business and Employment / 93

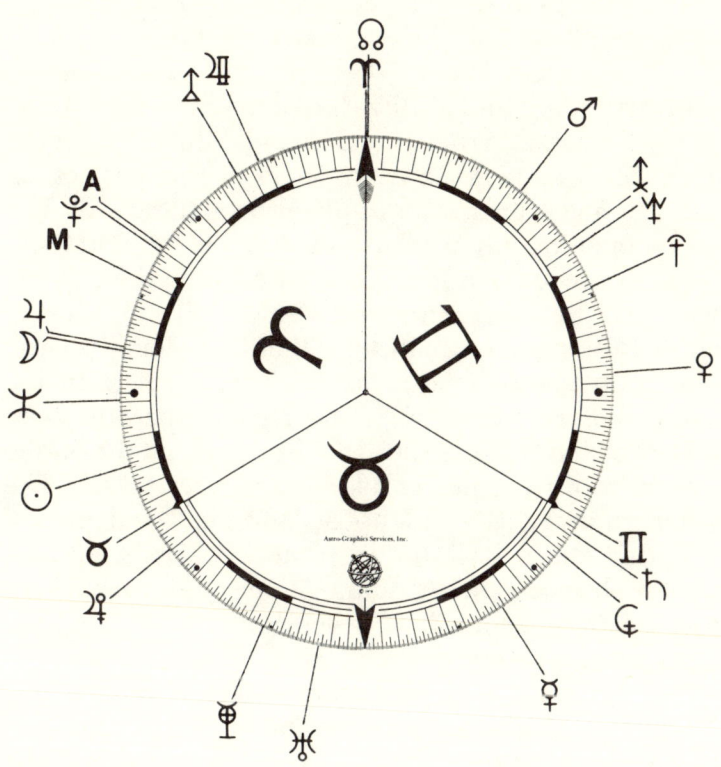

	Longitude	Latitude	Right Ascension	Declination
N. Node	29°VI59'	0°N00'	179° 59'	0°N00'
Cupido	1°SC53'	1°N05'	210° 05'	11°S07'
Hades	27°TA55'	1°S00'	55° 53'	18°N43'
Zeus	16°VI28'	0°N00'	167° 33'	5°N20'
Kronos	13°GE33'	0°N00'	72° 10'	22°N26'
Apollon	6°LI21'	0°N00'	185° 50'	2°S31'
Admetos	7°TA58'	0°N00'	35° 36'	14°N10'
Vulcanus	8°CN52'	0°N00'	99° 39'	23°N09'
Poseidon	22°LI52'	0°N00'	201° 09'	8°S54'
Ascendant	13°LI50'	0°N00'	192° 43'	5°S27'
Midheaven	16°CN00'	0°N00'	107° 21'	22°N29'

and her two sisters and was very nervous about the project. The restaurant stayed open for only four months and was sold six months after opening day.

The Ascendant and Midheaven of the chart are almost exactly the same as the Ascendant and Midheaven of the owner. He was personally involved in this project, as would be suggested by this duplication of the angles. The Sun on opening day was also conjunct his natal Moon. The most obvious difficult configuration in the chart is the square between Mars and Venus very close to the angles. Both planets are in signs that traditionally cause them problems and both are important rulers in the business chart. Venus rules the 1st and the 8th while Mars rules the 2nd and the 7th. The place and the public were in conflict, ruler of 1st square ruler of 7th. The owner changed the old house and the local people boycotted the restaurant in protest. There were also many problems with financing. At one point a necessary bank loan was delayed for several months causing the owner much anxiety. On the 90 degree dial the Moon is seen to be linked with this Mars — Venus square by a 22½ degree series aspect ($7/16$ and $3/16$). This symbolizes the conflicts over the "roots" of the house and the contributions of the three sisters to the general problems. In fact, the three sisters consistently put pressure on the owner at every important decision, and in the case of the decorating problems, persuaded him to follow their ideas. These sisters were of an eastern European background and had absolutely no idea what an American colonial house should look like. Their "bad taste" outraged the local public, many of whom were direct descendants of the early settlers in that area and knew a good deal about colonial decor.

In this event chart the Moon is almost exactly at the degree of a Mercury station in January of 1976, three months earlier, and within two degrees of a square to a

Uranus station in February, two months earlier. This emphasis of an unstable mundane configuration (Mercury station square Uranus station) demonstrates how such data might be used in both interpreting event charts and electing times for events. It should be noted that the Moon is also square the place of a previous solar eclipse and was about to be squared by another solar eclipse which occured a month after opening. Also in the event chart, as seen on the 90 degree dial, Mars and Venus (together) and Neptune are equidistant from the Aries point, an indication of weakness and unrealistic actions. This event chart does not show a harmonius linkage to mundane astrological factors.

This restaurant closed when transiting Saturn opposed the Moon and simultaneously tied into the Venus-Mars square by the 22½ degrees series of aspects (¹⁄₁₆ and ⁵⁄₁₆). It was sold when transiting Pluto was within a few minutes of conjunction to the Ascendant. Further examination of the 90 degree dial shows that Uranus, Admetos, and Jupiter are all very close to the Sun/Moon midpoint. In traditional astrology this shows up as Sun conjunct Jupiter and Admetos, opposite Uranus, and square to the Moon; a T-square. In this configuration Uranus suggests financial instability and the Moon and Jupiter (ruler of the 3rd) the control of financial matters by one of the sisters. This planetary picture, as seen on the 90 degree dial, adds to this interpretation the suggestion of sudden enemies (Sun/Moon = Uranus) and days on which nothing happens (Sun/Moon = Admetos). The combination further suggests that there was some sudden luck in narrow circumstances for only a few. This may have been true, the owner did sell out to a large restaurant chain and may have made some money on the deal. The employees did not fare so well. One final observation seems relevant. Pluto is very close to the Ascendant and is linked with Hades by sesquiquadrate (³⁄₈) and the Sun by 22½ degree aspect (⁷⁄₁₆) which sym-

The Timing of Events: Electional Astrology

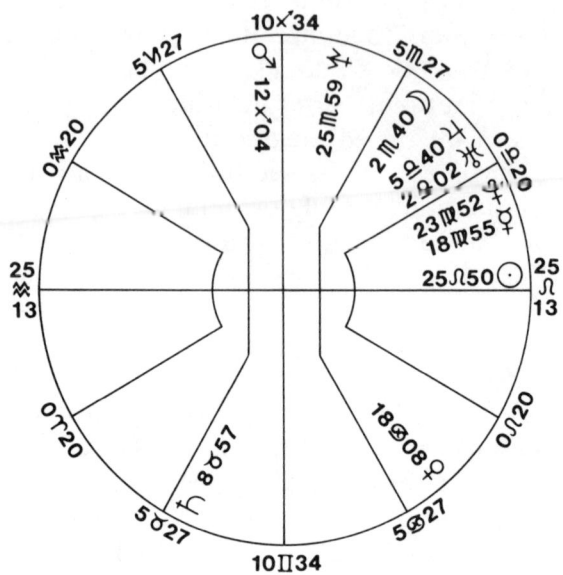

Chart 9

	Longitude	Latitude	Right Ascension	Declination
Sun	25°LE50'	0°N00'	148° 05'	12°N55'
Moon	2°SC40'	3°S28'	209° 14'	15°S40'
Mercury	18°VI55'	0°S06'	169° 47'	4°N18'
Venus	18°CN08'	0°S57'	109° 30'	21°N16'
Mars	12°SG04'	3°S14'	250° 06'	25°S27'
Jupiter	5°LI40'	1°N09'	185° 40'	1°S12'
Saturn	8°TA57'	2°S33'	37° 23'	12°N04'
Uranus	2°LI02'	0°N42'	182° 08'	0°S10'
Neptune	25°SC59'	1°N42'	234° 04'	17°S36'
Pluto	23°VI52'	15°N11'	180° 34'	16°N20'

Business and Employment / 97

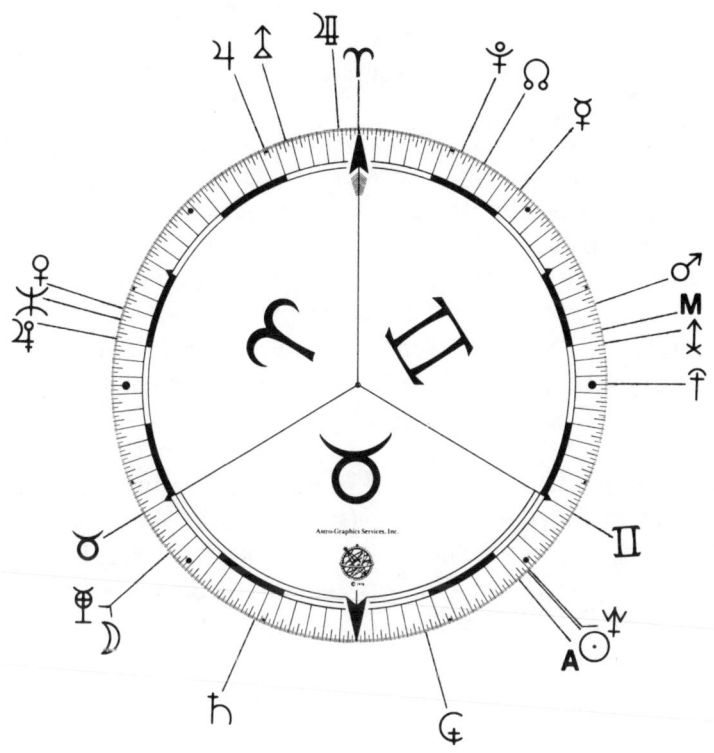

	Longitude	Latitude	Right Ascension	Declination
N. Node	22°PI26'	0°N00'	353° 03'	3°S00'
Cupido	19°LI48'	1°N00'	198° 40'	6°S49'
Hades	19°TA03'	0°S58'	46° 52'	16°N34'
Zeus	9°VI50'	0°N00'	161° 22'	7°N53'
Kronos	7°GE34'	0°N00'	65° 47'	21°N35'
Apollon	1°LI05'	0°N00'	180° 59'	0°S26'
Admetos	2°TA43' ℞	0°N00'	30° 30'	12°N25'
Vulcanus	4°CN22'	0°N00'	94° 46'	23°N22'
Poseidon	18°LI41'	0°N00'	197° 14'	7°S19'
Ascendant	25°AQ13'	0°N00'	327° 30'	13°S07'
Midheaven	10°SG34'	0°N00'	248° 58'	22°S02'

bolizes the restoration of a place that is old and decaying. In many respects the general situation was like an archaeological dig. When walls were removed, mud and straw were exposed between the boards.

Chart 8 is a re-incorporation chart for a business office, an employment agency. The time was elected and arrangements were made for the papers to be made official and stamped at a designated time. The office was re-incorporated because ownership arrangements were altered and a new office manager was installed. The elected time was created to symbolize financial power and strength, and to have strong connections to the birth chart of the new office manager.

The Sun and Jupiter, in conjunction, are placed powerfully in the 10th house with Jupiter particularly close to the the Midheaven. The Moon, ruler of the 10th, is located in the fourth in Capricorn opposite to these planets. Business is basically oppositional in nature, which is usually seen in the birth charts of successful business people. An opposition such as this serves to stimulate the entire chart. Venus, ruler of the 1st, is applying to a sextile of Uranus in the second, a good connection for a money making endeavor. Pluto is rising, rules the 2nd, and is in square to the Jupiter-Moon opposition suggesting some power struggles over large amounts of money. In a business such as this, events of this nature are not unusual. This T-square, or from another view Pluto at the midpoint of the Moon and Jupiter, suggest great power and big money. Note that the Moon is separating from the configuration and is applying to a trine of Mars. The other points of this configuration also have sextiles for balance. On the 90 degree chart we see the Midheaven near the midpoint of Jupiter and Pluto and the Moon and Jupiter at the midpoint of the Midheaven and the Sun. Uranus is in the 2nd, stationary in Scorpio and is also in trine to the Midheaven and in a close 22½ degree series aspect (5/16) to Jupiter, all of which suggest big money. In regard to financial matters, this chart emphasizes the appropriate symbols as best as was possible within the context of the other important considerations.

As mentioned, this election took into account the natal chart of the office manager. The electional Ascendant is exactly conjunct the manager's Sun indicating that she will easily dominate the situation. The Moon is in her natal 1st house and conjunct her Jupiter. The Sun is exactly trine her natal Venus in her 10th house indicating both pleasure and business success. Although this manager runs three offices, the office with this electional chart has become her base of operations. The office tends to do business with very large corporations and has been a financial success. Both this case study and the previous one, chart 7, have Pluto rising and in both cases changes in ownership occurred rather quickly from the time of "initiation". In the case at hand, the office was sold to the office manager about one year after re-incorporation, when the directed Midheaven came to the exact midpoint of Pluto and Jupiter.

The next example, chart 9, is that of the starting point of a small jazz/rock group. The chart was cast for the time that the four members first began playing music, in this case a rehearsal. The chart of first public performance is generally not useful because it seems to refer primarily to the events of that particular engagement. This group's origins had some of the qualities of an election. It was started on a day during which favorable aspects to Venus were forming in the organizer's chart. The band lasted about two years, not too bad in the music business, and was very progressive musically. There was a high level of abstraction in the music about 90% of which was improvised. The group developed a small following of intellectual types, played some interesting and somewhat prestigious jobs in New York City, recorded a record album which was never released, and finally disbanded in May of 1971 because of ego conflicts and economic problems.

The dominant aspect in this chart is the Sun-Neptune square. In fact, the very existence of the group depended on a belief that the group had a mission to perform, this information having been revealed through dreams and visions. When economic problems became overwhelming and began to weaken this belief, the band fell apart. The revolutionary nature of the band is symbolized by the conjunction of the ruler of the Ascendant, Uranus, with the ruler of the Midheaven, Jupiter. The musical objectives were always radical and with Mars near the Midheaven a pioneering element was prominent. Mars had retrograded earlier and was about five degrees before its first station suggesting a kind of prematurity — which, in retrospect, was the case. It appears that the moment a planet passes its station is a good indicator of readiness and maturity. This is, of course, most important when the planet is angular in the chart or is the significator of the event. Venus in the fifth sextile Mercury refers to the creativity of the group, which was considerable. Venus is also part of a grand quintile involving Uranus, Mars, Saturn, and the Ascendant. This structure suggests unusual, aggressive, and structural creativity. The Moon, ruler of the fifth, is opposite Admetos suggesting primitive creativity and blocked creativity, both being the case. There was a tendency to spend much musical time in one key centered around a basic drone and pulse. At times there were also no ideas, and forms and structures had to be relied on.

Saturn in Taurus, opposite the Moon in the 8th, shows the heavy economic problems the band had and its need to borrow money because of scarce resources. Admetos is also exactly opposite this Moon emphasizing the problem while Pluto is sesquiquadrate Saturn further stressing the economic situation of the group. The Midheaven, on the 90 degree dial, is closely linked to Zeus which underscores the tremendous creative urges of the band. Mars and Kronos are symmetrically grouped around this Midheaven and suggest that this band was a great leader and a creative leader. Pluto, on one side, and the Sun and Neptune on the other are also symmetrically grouped around this Midheaven. This suggests an involvement with strange and mysterious changes which was certainly true considering the lyrical content of the music that was performed. Most of the songs were about death and transformation. The group came to its end when transiting Saturn and transiting Uranus, together in a sesquiquadrate aspect, simultaneously aspected the Ascendant and Sun.

Employment Case Studies

The time that you begin a job has great significance. A chart cast for this time clearly spells out when promotions or cutbacks might occur and also describes the nature of your personal experience with that job. In some instances a newly hired employee may have a choice as to when he or she starts the job. With this situation electional astrology is potentially useful. Composite charts cast from the chart of the employee and the chart of the job are particularly revealing and could serve as a check on the selection of a start date and time. The starting time is the time that the person begins the actual job experience, usually the time from which offical records are kept. There are no other viable charts for employment with the exception of the chart for the time of the first interview, which refers primarily to the interview itself. The relationship between the interview chart and the official start chart should show strong connections with each other, but all practical predictive work should stem from the job start chart.

The Timing of Events: Electional Astrology

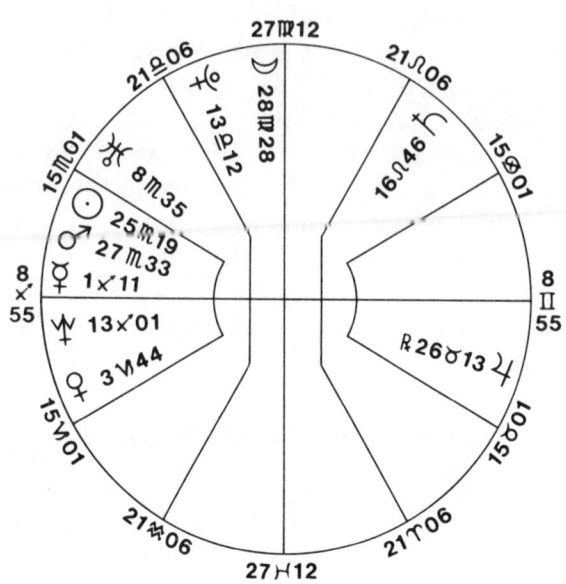

Chart 10

	Longitude	Latitude	Right Ascension	Declination
Sun	25°SC19'	0°N00'	232° 59'	19°S06'
Moon	28°VI28'	3°S01'	177° 24'	2°S10'
Mercury	1°SG11'	0°S59'	238° 50'	21°S22'
Venus	3°CP44'	2°S03'	274° 08'	25°S26'
Mars	27°SC33'	0°S11'	235° 13'	19°S48'
Jupiter	26°TA13' ℞	1°S08'	54° 11'	18°N13'
Saturn	16°LE46'	0°N45'	139° 28'	16°N32'
Uranus	8°SC35'	0°N26'	216° 21'	13°S57'
Neptune	13°SG01'	1°N27'	251° 47'	20°S55'
Pluto	13°LI12'	16°N35'	198° 37'	10°N04'

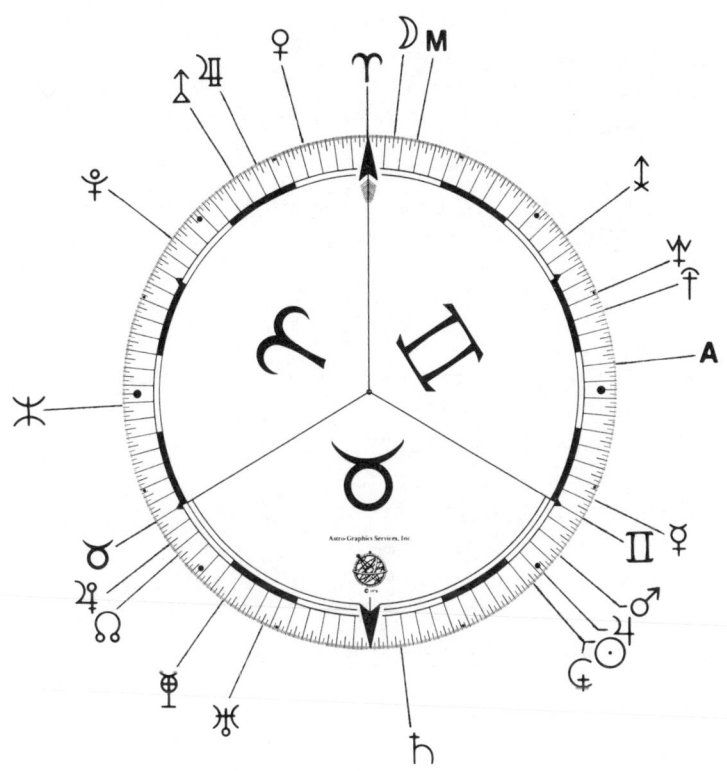

	Longitude	Latitude	Right Ascension	Declination
N. Node	2°SC14′	0°N00′	210° 03′	12°S15′
Cupido	1°SC32′	1°N03′	209° 45′	11°S02′
Hades	25°TA15′ ℞	1°S01′	53° 09′	18°N05′
Zeus	16°VI46′	0°N00′	167° 50′	5°N13′
Kronos	12°GE02′ ℞	0°N00′	70° 32′	22°N14′
Apollon	6°LI41′	0°N00′	186° 08′	2°S39′
Admetos	5°TA58′ ℞	0°N00′	33° 39′	13°N31′
Vulcanus	8°CN14′ ℞	0°N00′	98° 57′	23°N11′
Poseidon	23°LI07′	0°N00′	201° 23′	8°S59′
Ascendant	8°SG55′	0°N00′	247° 13′	21°S47′
Midheaven	27°VI12′	0°N00′	177° 26′	1°N07′

The Houses in Employment Charts

1. The general situation.

2. The paycheck.

3. Transportation factors, telephone and other communications.

4. The office or factory building.

5. Entertainment and pleasurable activities.

6. Sickness, schedule adjustments.

7. Persons encountered on the job.

8. Loans, company savings plans, shared profits.

9. Travel and transportation, legal matters.

10. The boss, management.

11. Group activities, associations.

12. Confinement, restrictions, plots and secret activities.

Chart 10 is that of the first day of work for a therapist/counselor at a special school for emotionally disturbed adolescents. The job lasted a year and a half, paid well, but involved long range commuting and many emotionally draining experiences, both with the students and with the fellow employees and directors. The job was made obsolete due to behind the scenes manipulations by one of the directors who was apparently angered by what he considered to be an affront to his sexuality and power. The employee in this case rejected the sexual advances of the director and developed a deep lack of respect for him — he sensed it and eliminated her job.

The chart shows a strong Moon and Neptune. The Moon in Virgo suggests health matters and associations with females. While on the job, the employee developed an interest in health and applied this interest to the job by paying a good deal of attention to the diets of the students. The Moon at the top of the chart also shows the maternal attitude toward the students that developed, particularly female students. Neptune rising in the 1st in Sagittarius indicates some confusion about the general situation and the fact that the property (Neptune rules the 4th house) was a significant factor in the job experience. The school was in an old and deteriorating house and its future was always uncertain. The two strongest planets in this chart, the Moon and Neptune, suggest that the experience of the job was a very emotional one, involving, the students, the directors, and fellow employees.

The conjunction of the Sun and Mars in the 12th house is the indicator of the secret power struggles and sexual tensions. The major struggles of the job involved two males with Sun positions in Aries and Scorpio. This Sun-Mars conjunction is opposed by Jupiter in Taurus, and interestingly, the one source of help in this job experience was through a male born with Sun in Taurus. On the 90 degree dial Hades is exactly linked to the Sun making this configuration particularly nasty. There were secret meetings that were central to this job experience and false rumors were spread. Good work was not given credit and many days were unpleasant. Further investigation on the 90 degree dial shows that Saturn forms an almost perfect 22½ degree series aspect (3/16) to the Ascendant. This suggest personal problems with authorities of an 8th house nature.

106 / The Timing of Events: Electional Astrology

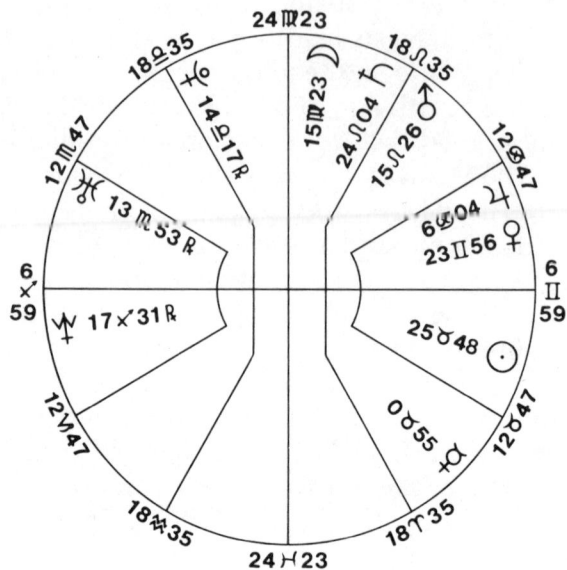

Chart 11

	Longitude	Latitude	Right Ascension	Declination
Sun	25°TA48'	0°N00'	53° 28'	19°N13'
Moon	15°VI23'	1°S42'	165° 53'	4°N12'
Mercury	0°TA55'	3°S05'	29° 52'	8°N54'
Venus	23°GE56'	1°N17'	83° 20'	24°N36'
Mars	15°LE26'	1°N42'	138° 26'	17°N50'
Jupiter	6°CN04'	0°N04'	96° 36'	23°N22'
Saturn	24°LE04'	1°N30'	146° 53'	14°N55'
Uranus	13°SC53' ℞	0°N24'	221° 33'	15°S38'
Neptune	17°SG31' ℞	1°N30'	256° 35'	21°S22'
Pluto	14°LI17' ℞	17°N31'	199° 58'	10°N32'

Business and Employment / 107

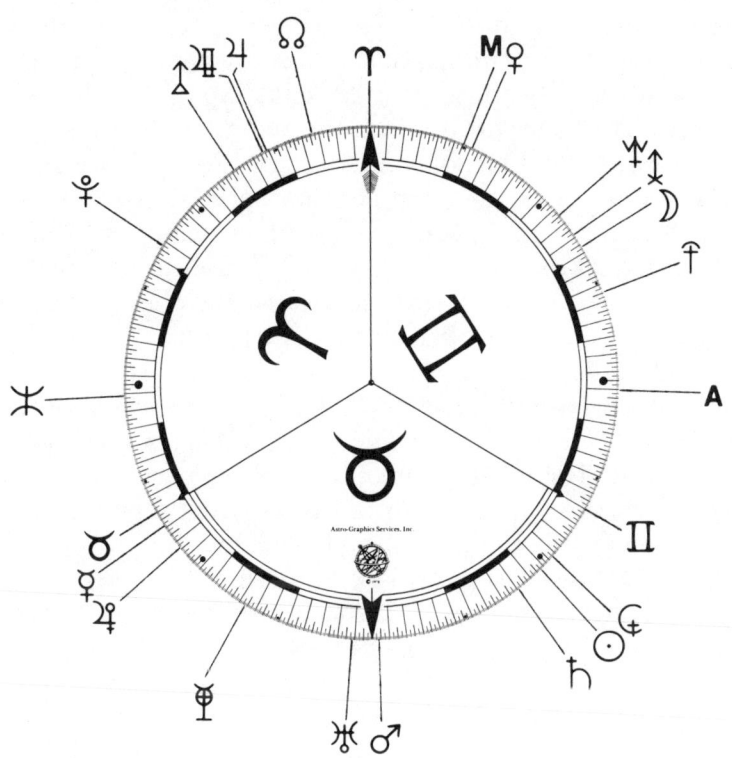

	Longitude	Latitude	Right Ascension	Declination
N. Node	3°LI21′	0°N00′	183° 04′	1°S20′
Cupido	2°SC29′ ℞	1°N06′	210° 41′	11°S18′
Hades	26°TA44′	0°S59′	54° 41′	18°N28′
Zeus	16°VI10′ ℞	0°N00′	167° 16′	5°N28′
Kronos	12°GE34′	0°N00′	71° 06′	22°N18′
Apollon	6°LI23′ ℞	0°N00′	185° 52′	2°S32′
Admetos	7°TA20′	0°N00′	34° 59′	13°N58′
Vulcanus	8°CN02′	0°N00′	98° 45′	23°N12′
Poseidon	23°LI06′ ℞	0°N00′	201° 22′	8°S59′
Ascendant	6°SG59′	0°N00′	245° 10′	21°S29′
Midheaven	24°VI23′	0°N00′	174° 51′	2°N14′

The Midheaven of this chart is close to the midpoint of Uranus and Saturn, a direct midpoint in this case. The two planets are symmetrically grouped around the Midheaven suggesting sudden quarrels and separations with others, especially those in authority. This midpoint is particularly powerful because the two planets are separated by a lower harmonic, in this case the 8th. Notice of job termination occurred in February of 1978 when Saturn, then retrograde, squared the charts Sun position. The last working day occured when transiting Saturn, now moving direct, was exactly square the chart's Jupiter and just one degree from the chart's Sun.

The next example, chart 11, is of the beginning of a three week musical engagement at a local lounge by a local band. The group started the job performing contemporary disco and ballad material with an emphasis on the vocals. At the end of the first week the drummer quit. This caused some quick adjustments and a new drummer joined the group with a saxophone player who was willing to work for low pay. By the end of the first night of the second week, the vocalists in the band developed severe throat problems and were unable to sing for the rest of the week. The band now played instrumental standards and much jazz. The new drummer had come from a punk rock band and added a primal touch to the old standards. At the start of the third week he was replaced with another drummer and the band reverted to vocal music. At this point the group was playing every possible musical style including Country and Western, Jazz, Rock and Roll, and Polkas. The engagement was completely successful from both the management's and audience's points of view.

The engagement ran from Tuesdays to Saturdays of each week but a large number of aspects to the job chart fell on the Monday of the second week. It was on this day that the first drummer quit suddenly because of a scheduling conflict in his life. Transiting Mercury was sesquiquadrate the charts Midheaven on that Monday and transiting Venus entered the midpoint of the charts Mars-Uranus square. More direct information is gained from a look at the 90 degree chart. The dominant configuration of this chart is the Midheaven-Venus and the Jupiter-Apollon grouping around the Aries point of the chart. This suggests public and artistic success in more ways than one. Notice also that Mars and Uranus are also grouped around this Aries axis suggesting sudden rupture and stressful change or conflict. On the Monday of the second week, transiting Venus was passing through the center of this planetary picture. Venus rules the sixth house of employees and scheduling. The Midheaven, which moves about one degree per day, also arrived at this Aries point on this day.

When transiting Mars conjuncted the chart's Saturn, ruler of the second, there was a short delay and a conflict over payment. On one of the nights the transiting Moon tied into the Midheaven-Venus linkage. Exactly to the minute an appropriate event occured, a couple wanted the band to announce the fact that they were getting married. The job itself ended within five minutes time of an exact conjunction of the transiting Moon with the charts Sun. This kind of detail work can be done on any event chart but it is most useful with a short lived event. Obsession with details can draw an interpreter away from the main issues and it is not my intention to encourage such meticulous work except where it is appropriate or necessary.

Chart 12 is that of the starting time of a lifetime career at a public utility. The job was that of electrical engineer. The durability of this situation is shown by the fixed sign Ascendant, Jupiter (ruler of the 6th house) which is angular and in a fixed sign, and the Midheaven in close aspect to Mars and Saturn. In this case the pressure

110 / The Timing of Events: Electional Astrology

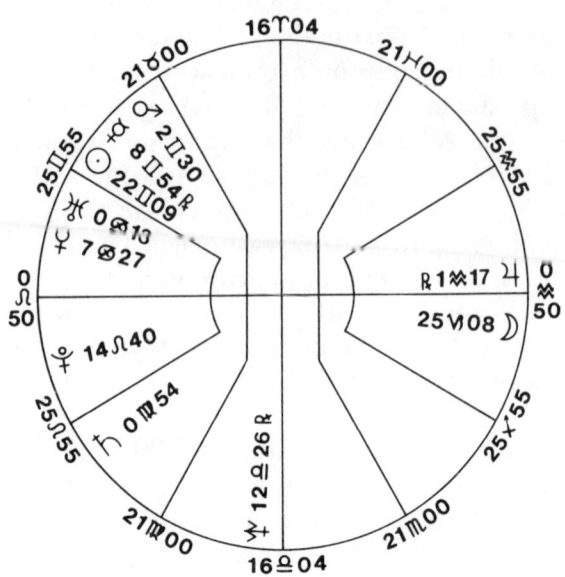

Chart 12

	Longitude	Latitude	Right Ascension	Declination
Sun	22°GE09′	0°N00′	81° 28′	23°N13′
Moon	25°CP08′	5°S05′	298° 07′	26°S07′
Mercury	8°GE54′ ℞	4°S13′	67° 52′	17°N38′
Venus	7°CN27′	1°N01′	98° 11′	24°N15′
Mars	2°GE30′	0°S00′	60° 26′	20°N40′
Jupiter	1°AQ17′ ℞	0°S23′	303° 37′	20°S15′
Saturn	0°VI54′	1°N39′	153° 33′	12°N43′
Uranus	0°CN13′	0°N13′	90° 14′	23°N40′
Neptune	12°LI26′ ℞	1°N36′	192° 03′	3°S26′
Pluto	14°LE40′	7°N39′	139° 34′	23°N45′

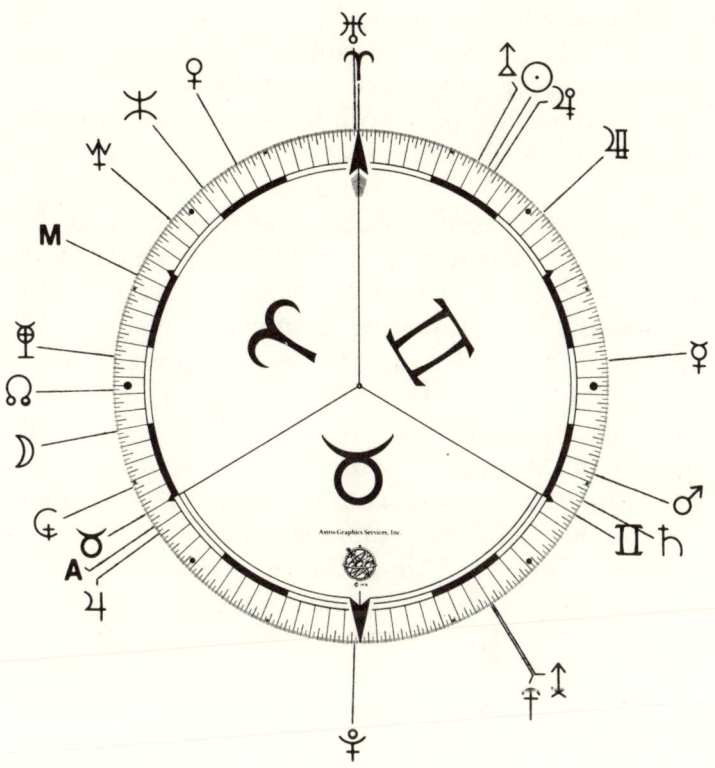

	Longitude	Latitude	Right Ascension	Declination
N. Node	22°AR47'	0°N00'	21° 04'	8°N52'
Cupido	21°VI41'	0°N44'	172° 39'	3°N59'
Hades	28°AR24'	0°S44'	26° 40'	10°N13'
Zeus	23°LE01'	0°N00'	145° 21'	13°N51'
Kronos	23°TA00'	0°N00'	50° 36'	18°N32'
Apollon	18°VI07'	0°N00'	169° 05'	4°N42'
Admetos	20°AR54'	0°N00'	19° 18'	8°N09'
Vulcanus	22°GE48'	0°N00'	82° 09'	23°N15'
Poseidon	8°LI48' ℞	0°N00'	188° 05'	3°S29'
Ascendant	0°LE50'	0°N00'	123° 03'	19°N59'
Midheaven	16°AR04'	0°N00'	14° 48'	6°N19'

between Mars and Saturn symbolizes the fact that the job was basically problem solving, rather than symbolizing problems with the job itself. The chart is compatible with the natal chart of the employee, particularly the Ascendant of the job chart sextile his natal Saturn-Jupiter conjunction in his 6th house and the job chart Sun trine his natal Sun.

Major promotions in this job show very clearly and it is this aspect that suggested its inclusion as a case study. The first promotion to assistant engineer, occured after two years of work. Transiting Jupiter was near the Midheaven, and Saturn by solar arc direction was close to squaring Mars, ruler of the 10th house. When this employee was made engineer, transiting Jupiter was stationary on the Midheaven while Mars by solar arc formed a sesquiquadrate to Jupiter. At the time of promotion to senior engineer, Jupiter was again conjunct the Midheaven exactly and this time Mars was doing so also. The Sun by solar arc was near a square to the Midheaven and a semisquare to Mars, the average of these two arcs almost exactly equaling the arc of the event. In this chart Mars and Jupiter are in trine to each other. This suggests, through Mars' rulership of the Midheaven, that promotions would come about in this job, but especially so when transiting Mars and Jupiter were conjunct on the Midheaven of this chart, the time that promotion to senior engineer occurred.

Retirement occurred after 31 years, 3 months, and 15 days and was symbolized by the solar arc directed Midheaven passing square to Pluto and semisquare to Uranus. These directions were mathematically exact about a year before the event occurred. A large number of other appropriate symbols of the event were mathematically exact much closer to the actual date such as the solar arc directed Sun passing through the midpoint of Admetos and the mean node (both in the 10th house), and Saturn moving to the square of Uranus. Probably the most significant transits which occurred at this time were Pluto exactly opposite the charts Admetos in the 10th house and Saturn square the charts Uranus, exactly duplicating the solar arc direction mentioned above.

Chapter 7

Further Studies

Charts for events that involve many people, particularly events of a public nature, often show strong ties to previous eclipse degrees and planetary stations. When these ties are favorable, the event tends to be successful, when not, failure is a possibility. In the chapter on business charts this point was made and some examples were given. In the first part of this chapter we will look at charts for major public events, keeping this mundane perspective in mind as we analyze the planets at the time of commencement. The second half of the chapter will deal with micro-elections; the use of Meridian and Horizon crossings of natal planets and angles, parans, and the use of this information in gambling.

The first example, chart 13, is that of the "airing" of the first episode of the very successful television program *M.A.S.H.* This occured on September 17, 1972, a Sunday evening, at 8:00 PM Eastern Daylight Time. Time zones further west probably aired the show at 8:00 PM their time (later) but it seems reasonable to work with the chart for the region where it made its very first appearance in time — the eastern United states. The chart presented was cast for New York City. The angles for this chart will vary somewhat depending on what city or town one would choose. Boston would have a slightly later Midheaven and Ascendant and Pittsburgh earlier angles. However, regardless of where you were in the Eastern Standard Time Zone at its moment of public birth, *M.A.S.H.* would have Jupiter and the Moon placed near the top of the chart. They are the only elevated planets and they symbolize public success. In fact, in the vicinity of New York and Philadelphia, the maximum population region, the Midheaven is close to the midpoint of the Moon and Jupiter.

Further examination of this interesting chart confirms some of the basic principles of electional astrology. The Sun is separating from a conjunction with Mars and Mercury and a square to Saturn. The show had its problems, but I don't think they were as pressing as they would have been if the show had been aired while the Sun was applying to this tense configuration. Crises are generally more manageable when hard aspects are separating. The progressed or directed Sun did not move into these planets, it already passed them and was on its way to a square with Jupiter. *M.A.S.H.* was not a time bomb.

The stellium in the 6th house symbolizes scheduling problems. This program experienced seven time slot changes, the rotation of 17 writers and the loss of half the original cast. The symbolism of the planets in this stellium fits the nature of the program which was about a Mobile (Mercury) Army (Mars-Virgo) Surgical Hospital (planets in Virgo and 6th house, Sun applying to a conjunction with Pluto). If a show that did not fit this symbolism so well was aired at this time, it may not have become so very successful. The presence of Saturn in Gemini in square to the stellium in Virgo, besides suggesting the schedule problems already mentioned, suggests the need for depth and seriousness which the show certainly had. Interestingly, the first colonel in the program, the character Henry Blake, was killed while traveling out of Korea in a plane. Perhaps this is suggested by Saturn square to Mars and Mercury, the violent loss of an authority while in transit, even though it was a fiction. Finally, this stellium in Virgo is trined, an

116 / The Timing of Events: Electional Astrology

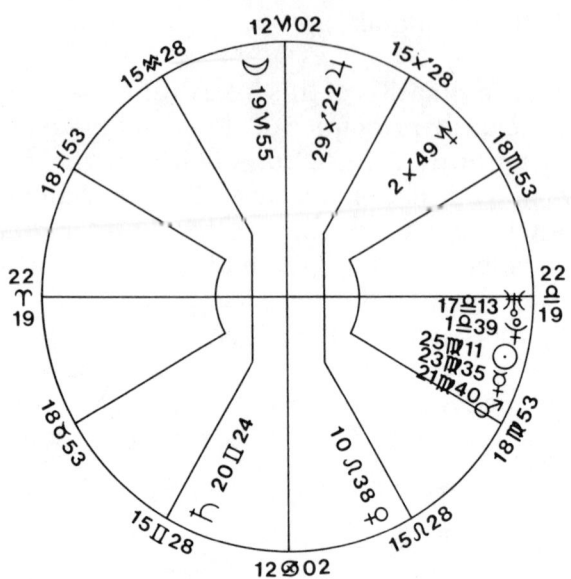

Chart 13

	Longitude	Latitude	Right Ascension	Declination
Sun	25°VI11'	0°N00'	175° 34'	1°N55'
Moon	19°CP55'	0°S23'	291° 37'	22°S20'
Mercury	23°VI35'	1°N38'	174° 45'	4°N02'
Venus	10°LE38'	1°S06'	132° 47'	16°N30'
Mars	21°VI40'	1°N00'	172° 44'	4°N13'
Jupiter	29°SG22'	0°S00'	269° 18'	23°S27'
Saturn	20°GE24'	1°S36'	79° 41'	21°N30'
Uranus	17°LI13'	0°N36'	196° 07'	6°S12'
Neptune	2°SG49'	1°N37'	241° 05'	19°S09'
Pluto	1°LI39'	15°N50'	187° 56'	13°N51'

Further Studies / 117

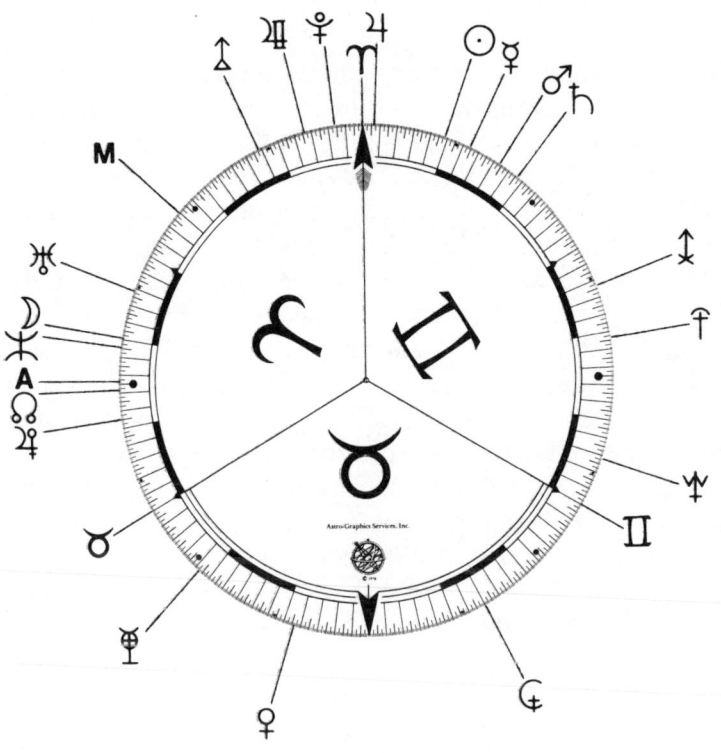

	Longitude	Latitude	Right Ascension	Declination
N. Node	22°CP48'	0°N00'	294° 37'	21°S31'
Cupido	24°LI31'	1°N01'	203° 06'	8°S33'
Hades	21°TA59' ℞	0°S59'	49° 50'	17°N19'
Zeus	12°VI45'	0°N00'	164° 06'	6°N47'
Kronos	9°GE43' ℞	0°N00'	68° 03'	21°N55'
Apollon	3°LI22'	0°N00'	183° 05'	1°S20'
Admetos	4°TA17' ℞	0°N00'	32° 01'	12°N57'
Vulcanus	6°CN12'	0°N00'	96° 45'	23°N18'
Poseidon	20°LI26'	0°N00'	198° 53'	7°S59'
Ascendant	22°AR19'	0°N00'	20° 39'	8°N41'
Midheaven	12°CP02'	0°N00'	283° 04'	22°S54'

applying trine, to the elevated Moon and in square to Jupiter, both of which certainly compensated for the other pressures.

Of particular interest are the elements of this chart that link it to mundane events. The Moon is located nearly opposite the previous lunar eclipse which occured on July 10, 1972 at 18 Cancer 37. Since this was a lunar eclipse, the Moon was actually conjunct the place of the Moon at the time of the eclipse. The Sun is very closely trine to the January 16, 1972 eclipse which occured at 25 Capricorn 25, and Venus is also nearly exactly conjunct the degree of Mercury's station in August 1972 at 10 Leo 31. Mars in the event chart is sextile the position of Mars in the Cancer solar ingress chart previous to the event and is trine to the Aries solar ingress Mars position before that. Since Aries is on the Ascendant of this event chart, and is ruled by Mars, this fact may be of great importance along with the eclipse linkages noted above.

Two other elements of this chart are worth noting. The Moon is in conjunction with its node; expressed another way it was just about to cross the ecliptic from south to north. Perhaps this amplifies its power in an event chart such as this. Secondly, the planet Jupiter, which as we have already noted is like the Moon elevated and close to the Midheaven, is also nearly conjunct the first degree of Capricorn. Planets at the Cardinal points, or at 15 degrees of the fixed signs, are linked to the world according to many of the ancient and modern astrologers. Of even greater significance is the symmetry that Jupiter and Pluto form around the Cardinal points, visible on the 90 degree dial. This is expressed as Jupiter/Pluto = Aries, and this is one of the best combinations for outstanding success on a large scale.

In 1979 and 1980 many politicians announced their candidacy for the office of the President of the United

States. Each made sure that the press knew on what day this announcement was to occur and each each received a good deal of publicity. This kind of ritual formality has great meaning when looked at astrologically, the similarity to the wedding ceremony being the most obvious. In any case, of all those who ran only one, Ronald Reagan, won the race. In the following paragraphs we will look at planetary configurations on the day that each of the contenders announced their candidacy. Since announcement times were not readily available, I have used charts cast for noon, Washington, D.C.

On January 24, 1979 John Connally made his announcement. The Sun and Mars were in conjunction near the 4th degree of Aquarius and were exactly opposed by Jupiter in Leo. He had a rather large "war chest" for his campaign. The Moon was tied to a conjunction with Venus and Neptune and was square to Saturn, the latter not being a very good omen in any election. Only Mercury at 24 degrees of Capricorn was in close aspect to a previous eclipse, in this case by sextile. This chart is a time bomb. Transiting Saturn by late 1979 would square the Moon, Venus and Neptune and sesquiquadrate the Sun and Mars and semisquare Jupiter. He dropped out on March 9, 1980.

George Bush announced on May 1, 1979 with the Sun at 11 degrees of Taurus in wide sextile to a previous eclipse at 7½ degrees of Pisces. The Moon was square to Pluto on one side and square to Mercury and Mars on the other. This is not so bad as it might seem — it suggests assertiveness and fight, something needed in a presidential campaign. Bush was born with the Sun in Gemini and the condition of Mercury would be of great importance in anything that he might do. The Sun in this announcement chart is trine to Saturn in Virgo and it apparently was comfortable (and opportunistic) for him to reverse some positions and become more of a servant.

Robert Dole announced on May 14, 1979 with the Sun separating from an opposition with Uranus and closely trine the position of a recent Lunar eclipse. The Moon may have been void of course depending on the time of his announcement. He withdrew on March 15, 1980 citing lack of money, management and manpower as his reasons. One would expect a debilitated Sun and Saturn in the chart to symbolize this and they do in a very subtle, but no less powerful, way. The Sun, Saturn and Neptune are all linked tightly by 7th harmonic aspects. Saturn and Neptune are almost exactly biseptile and the Sun and Saturn are just a degree off this same aspect. Saturn stands at the midpoint of the Sun and Neptune which are linked by triseptile. Again, midpoint configurations involving the lower harmonics (aspects normally employed in astrology plus the quintile, septile and novile) can be extremely powerful.

Howard Baker made his announcement on November 1, 1979 on a day when Mars and Uranus were in close square and the Sun was semisquare Saturn, neither of which are indications of helpful and cooperative circumstances. The Moon stood near the midpoint of this Mars-Uranus square in early Aries. There were no important linkages with the previous solar eclipse but there was a wide trine of the Sun to the solar eclipse earlier in the year and also to the position of the previous lunar eclipse.

Ted Kennedy announced on November 7, 1979 with Mercury semisquare Pluto, Mars semisextile Saturn and the Moon in square to Saturn and possibly void of course. The Sun was in trine to the position of the previous Lunar eclipse at 13 degrees of Pisces. Kennedy made his announcement around 10 or 11 AM giving a possible Capricorn Ascendant and a late Libra or early Scorpio Midheaven. Venus in close conjunction with Mercury suggests the beautiful rhetoric which was heard during and especially at the very end of his campaign. But Mercury was just about to go retrograde and did so on the very next day, the day on which Jerry Brown made his official bid. Although this was the second time Brown campaigned for the Presidency, this retrograde obviously didn't work for him. The Moon on this day was also applying to a square with Pluto and positioned in Cancer. Outside of the Sun widely trine to the previous Lunar eclipse, there was nothing on these two days that seemed to be "winning" for these two men. The Mars-Saturn semisextile mentioned above also tied exactly into Brown's natal seventh house Jupiter, scarcely a good omen of public success.

John Anderson made his announcement for an independent candidacy on April 24, 1980. The Moon was probably in early Virgo separating from Jupiter and applying to Saturn, symbolic of a good start but a bad finish. The Sun was nearly opposite the midpoint of the Saturn-Neptune square and was sesquiquadrate both these points, very much like Dole's chart but involving the eighth harmonic instead of the seventh. Venus was also involved in this planetary picture and was square to Saturn, opposite Neptune and semisquare the Sun. The Sun and Moon do not show successful management and organization in this chart. Mars, located very close to an opposition with the previous Solar eclipse at 27 Aquarius, suggests a state of war with the "world", not a good omen of success.

Ronald Reagan announced on November 13, 1979. This appears as chart 14. Mercury was retrograde—but this was his third bid for the Presidency. The Sun on this day was in nearly exact conjunction with Uranus. Exact conjunctions are very powerful and this one was particularly in line (symbolically) with his campaign theme of revolutionizing the budget of the government. The Moon was separating from a conjunction with Jupiter and moving towards a square with Neptune and a sextile

The Timing of Events: Electional Astrology

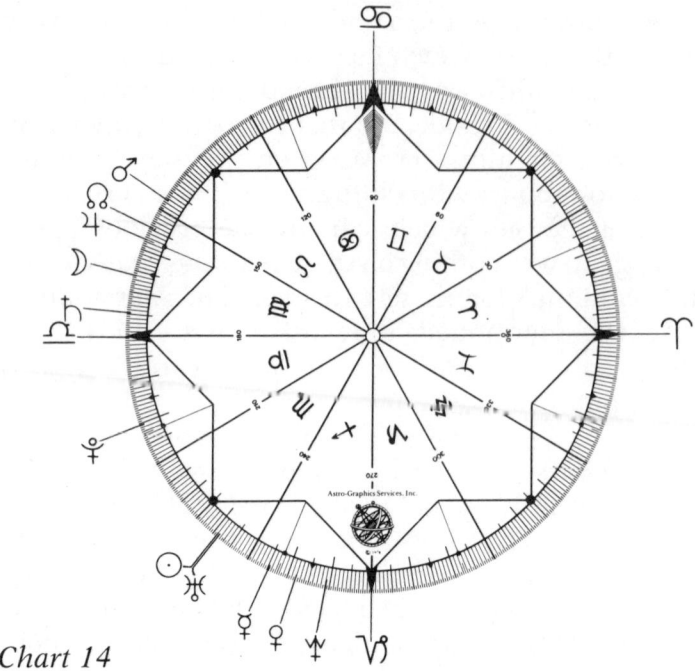

Chart 14

	Long.	Decl.		Long.	Decl.
Sun	21°SC01'	18°S01'	Saturn	24°VI31'	3°N58'
Moon	16°VI02'	6°N22'	Uranus	21°SC18'	17°S49'
Mercury	4°SG16' ℞	22°S26'	Neptune	19°SG10'	21°S39'
Venus	11°SG51'	22°S51'	Pluto	20°LI22'	7°N30'
Mars	27°LE17'	14°N10'	N. Node	4°VI26'	9°N53'
Jupiter	7°VI29'	9°N37'			

with the Sun-Uranus conjunction. According to the New York Times, Reagan made his announcement during the evening in New York City at the Hilton. This would put the Moon fairly close to completing a semisextile fan involving Pluto, Sun-Uranus, and Neptune. This suggests a tight organization for the most part. Mars was conjunct the degree of the previous Solar eclipse which occured at 29 Leo, near the fixed star Regulus—traditionally ascribed to royalty. The Moon in turn was close to opposition with the degree of the previous Lunar

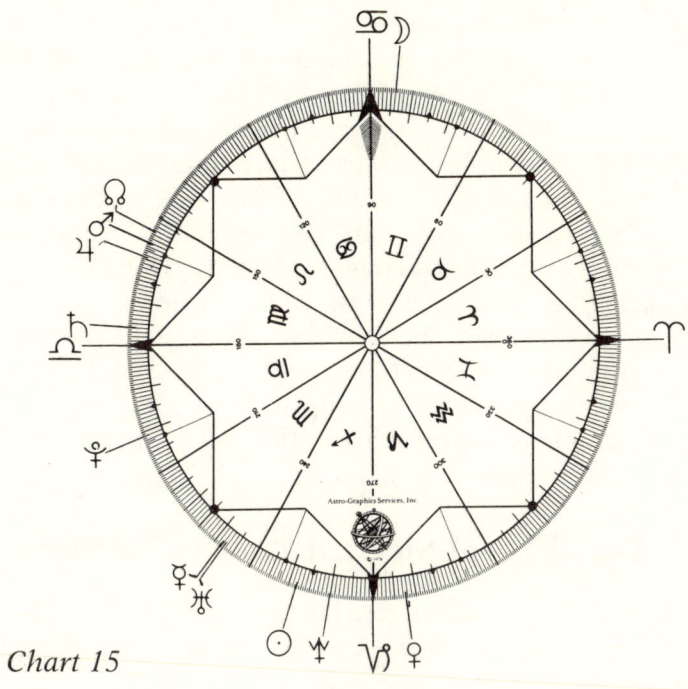

Chart 15

	Long.	Decl.		Long.	Decl.
Sun	11°SG57'	22°S14'	Saturn	26°VI02'	3°N27'
Moon	23°GE53'	18°N37'	Uranus	22°SC34'	18°S09'
Mercury	21°SC46'	15°S45'	Neptune	19°SG55'	21°S43'
Venus	7°CP37'	24°S37'	Pluto	21°LI02'	7°N23'
Mars	6°VI11'	11°N26'	N. Node	3°VI21'	10°N17'
Jupiter	9°VI29'	8°N57'			

eclipse at 13 Pisces. Actually the Moon was near the Sun's position in this eclipse. Overall this is a very powerful chart, undoubtedly the most powerful of those we have already seen. Although I was not able to obtain the exact time of the announcement, it probably occured around 8 PM or so with Aries at the Midheaven. The 10th house ruler, Mars, conjunct the degree of the previous eclipse seems especially potent.

Finally, Jimmy Carter announced his candidacy on

December 4, 1979. Unlike Reagan's big bash at the Hilton during prime time, Carter announced quietly sometime during the day at the White House. Again I was unable to locate an exact time for the event which appears as chart 15. On this day the Moon was square to Saturn, a very bad omen. Mars was semisquare Pluto and Venus was semisquare Uranus, both unstable aspects. Mercury in conjunction with Uranus suggested the need for a radical form of communication or some radically new ideas, but these never surfaced. The Sun was positioned in square to the previous Lunar eclipse at 13 Pisces and nothing aspects the previous Solar eclipse. In general this is a strained and frustrating chart, reflecting the nature and destiny of his losing campaign.

The Use of Local Sidereal Time in Elections

A further refinement in the increasingly complex world of electional astrology is the use of local sidereal time. At one moment every day, the first point of Aries (the intersection of the ecliptic and the equator — the beginning of the tropical zodiac) crosses your local Meridian. A chart cast for this time would have zero degrees of Aries at the Midheaven. The sidereal time for this event is always 0 hours 0 minutes and 0 seconds. The Ascendant would depend on your latitude. Suppose that at your birth you had Jupiter at 13 degrees of Aries and you wanted to elect a time for yourself that had 13 degrees of Aries at the Midheaven. As was demonstrated in a previous chapter, you could simply find the sidereal time that this would occur, make a calculation and arrive at the correct clock time for this event. In that same chapter I also pointed out that regarding the actual bodily risings of planets, this approach is not completely accurate, especially for Pluto. What you need to know is the local sidereal time (same as the right ascension of the Midheaven—RAMC) when each of your natal planets actually crosses the Meridian (upper and lower) and the

Horizon (rising and setting). Fortunately this information is now available from computing services under the name parans.

Technically a paran is a simultaneous crossing of either the Meridian or Horizon by two or more planets. Paran is a shortening of the word paranatellonta which was used by ancient astronomers and astrologers to denote simultaneous risings of planets, stars or constellations. A paran is more powerful than a single planet's crossing of one of the angles and as such may be useful information in the electional process. For example, in my natal chart I have a triple paran which occurs at about 12 hours and 42 minutes of local sidereal time. Every day at this time my natal Jupiter rises, natal Neptune culminates and natal Venus sets. Every day at this time (which occurs 4 minutes earlier each day) I am in a good mood, usually feeling sociable and often at my best. If I am at a party or with a group, this time often coincides with a peak of social excitement. If I leave my house at this time to go to a social event, it almost always turns out favorably. Knowledge of this diurnal rhythm has been a great aid in the often tedious selection of a time to commence an event of a personal nature. I should also point out that I have other parans in my chart which are not very good and these I avoid when electing a time.

For many years I studied my diurnal life experiences in the following way. I used a watch with a built-in 12 hour stopwatch and alarm. I would set the alarm to go off at the moment that zero degrees Aries crossed my local meridian. When the alarm rang, I would start the stopwatch. Every four minutes of time would then equal roughly one degree of movement at the Meridian. One hour on the stopwatch would correspond to about 15 degrees of Aries, two hours would be the sign change into Taurus. Essentially, the rotation of the Earth was being timed. But there are two major problems with this approach and several other significant limitations. First, the Earth rotates once every 23 hours 56 minutes and 4 seconds. By the time the stopwatch reaches 12 hours, the time is off by two minutes. The daily alarm must be reset four minutes earlier every day and the time read on the stopwatch must be increased (mentally with digital watches) at the rate of one minute every six hours. Second, ecliptic sign crossings at the Meridian do not occur at even sidereal times. What I noticed though is interesting and warrants further study. When observing the movements and activities of large numbers of people (in restaurants, at parties, etc.) a change of "sign" on the equator (every two hours) very often coincided with a shift in the social dynamics around me. People *en masse* tend to respond to astrological events like schools of fish and this is easily seen when observing the actual risings and culminations (and their counterparts—lower culmination and settings) of the planets themselves. I was surprised to see shifts occur when equatorial "signs" changed at the Meridian. More observation must take place before I can be assured that this is a viable phenomena.

Using a separate watch to time the rotation of the Earth — or the local sidereal time — is another possibility. Simply create graphs for each month that allow an easy determination of the local time that zero degrees of Aries is at the Midheaven. Look up the time that this took place or will take place, look at the present time, and set the watch accordingly. For example, if you know that zero degrees of Aries was at the Midheaven at 7:45 this morning and it is now 2:45 in the afternoon, take the difference between these two times, which is seven hours, and set your watch for seven o'clock. I use a laminated card which contains all the Horizon and Meridian crossings for my natal chart. Periodically one can simply check the card, look at the clock and either study personal reality or use the information to make mini-elections. A further refinement would be to set a watch to run four minutes fast which would make the daily adjustment less of a bother. Perhaps a digital sidereal watch will some day be manufactured. It should not only time the rotation of the Earth accurately at your local meridian, but it should store in its memory the sidereal times of all the planet crossings in your natal chart, these being shown on the watch face by symbol at the correct time.

A few comments on my own experiences using this kind of information may be appropriate. The sidereal time of your birth (when your natal Midheaven is at the local Meridian or Midheaven) is a good time to begin personal projects. At that time you are usually "in tune" with yourself. A good time to eat (feeding time) is when your natal Moon is at a crossing point. You tend to be dominant and get the attention of others when natal Mars or Sun are at crossing points. Lay low while Saturn is prominent, or work in private. I have noticed that the range or orb in time of most crossings is about 15 minutes, 7½ on each side of the actual time of the event. Meridian and Horizon crossings appear to be considerably more potent than squares to the Meridian and Prime Vertical transits.

Now let's take this approach a step further. Suppose that transiting Saturn is at 10 degrees of Libra and you were born with a 10 degree Libra Midheaven. When the sidereal time at your locality reads about 6 hours and 44 minutes, transiting Saturn and your natal Midheaven will both be crossing the local Meridian. This is double jeopardy. You should not use this time to begin a short term frivolous project. The use of a combination of natal crossing and paran information, plus the daily transiting information, is not only more complete, but more complicated. Due to the rapid motion of the Moon this data must be updated continually to be absolutely accurate. Two solutions are possible. First you can use the *Natural Cycles Almanac* as a handy (and quite accurate) way to see what is happening on an hourly basis. My friend Barry Orr has devised a clear overlay of one's natal crossings which, when placed over the one month page of the almanac, gives plenty of information in graphic form. The second solution, also pioneered by Barry, is a computer print-out which combines the crossing times of the daily planets and those of your own. A further refinement is a listing of the clock times of the day that each crossing occurs. With a list like this, the many parans occur each day will be seen easily. My experience with this kind of information indicates that it is essential for making micro-elections. Quick electional timing is extremely useful for gambling activities and in deciding when to make a move at partys or during business and other meetings.

And now on to gambling, the ultimate test of electional astrology. Many systems for the various kinds of gambling activities have been proposed, but the fact still remains—how many astrologers have become rich from gambling by using astrology? I know of none. Winning in something like a business or a marriage is relatively simple. First, to succeed you must know what you are doing and how to do it right. Second, when you make errors you correct them—and there is usually plenty of time for this. If you wish you can use astrology to further your chances for success and avoid pitfalls. With casino gambling and lotteries there is less to know and more to lose. There is usually less or even no time to make corrections so your timing had better be right. Horse racing is somewhat different. There is much to know (the horse's and jockey's record, the condition of the track, the particular race, etc.) and some people do quite well without astrology. The same could be said of card games where good counters can beat the odds. But the risks are still high and the opportunity to make corrections is low or even non-existent. Astrology can be applied to these situations successfully but certain conditions must be met.

The following are the main elements of my gambling system. It has been used successfully when all conditions have been met.

1. Do not attempt to gamble on a day, or even during a week when your natal chart (specifically, points symbolic of money) does not show success. Good aspects to and from Venus, Jupiter, Sun, Mars, and Uranus are also necessary. Watch the transiting midpoints, especially that of Jupiter and Uranus.

2. Once you have selected a day to gamble, make a listing of exactly when (to the minute) transits of the Moon and the midpoints of the Moon and the other planets contact sensitive points in your natal chart during the period you will be gambling. These times will serve as background information to the material assembled in the next step.

3. Using one of the methods described previously, know when the rotating Earth (local sidereal time) is in a favorable position for you. Your natal Jupiter, Sun or second or fifth house cusp just rising or culminating might be a good time to make a move, assuming that no natal afflicitions are prominent. With experience you will notice that certain areas of your chart crossing the Meridian of Horizon consistently produce good, or perhaps bad, results.

4. Use a 45 degree midpoint sort of your natal chart and notice where favorable midpoints and unfavorable midpoints are located. I have had good luck using the Uranian planets here. Gamble when the transiting Midheaven is linked by either

conjunction, opposition, square or semi- and sesquisquare to these points. If the time of such a transit coincides with the time of a lunar stimulation and the crossing of the Horizon or Meridian of a favorable planet or important degree in the chart, you will tend to win at that time.

My friend and student, Joe Lurelli, has created a system which is considerably more complex in some ways—but it has allowed him to win consistently at the card table in Atlantic City. He begins with his natal chart which includes the Trans-Neptunian planets of the Uranian system. The Sun, Jupiter, Apollon, Venus and Uranus are considered favorable. All combinations (midpoints and sums) of these planets and their contacts with his natal Midheaven and Moon are calculated. He next does the same for his solar arc directed natal chart for the present date. Finally, the current transits are included and all three charts are overlayed and similar points determined from a combination of all three. Once all these points have been calculated (and there are hundreds of them), they are put into a 45 degree mode and arranged in sequence. When two or more adjacent favorable zones are activated by the local transiting Midheaven, he plays cards, if only for a minute or two. By consistently playing only when some "good" combination of natal, directed and transiting planets are activated by the transiting Midheaven he has continued to win. In the near future computers will be programmed to handle these very tedious calculations.

Chapter 8

Recapitulation

The basic principles of electional astrology can be applied to many events and projects in modern life. The date and time on which this particular writing project began was elected. Following is a summary of the successive stages of the electional process with the electional chart of this book (chart 16) as an example.

1. The day on which the election will be determined should be carefully selected to insure that the astrologer's judgement is at its best.

The elected time to actively start writing was calculated two days after transiting Saturn had formed a sextile to the ruler of my third house which is positioned in Gemini. This insured that the electional process would proceed carefully. The actual work involved in electing a time is very much 3rd house/Mercury work and it is important that these symbols are not afflicted at the time that crucial judgements are being made. Attention to 9th house symbols is also important as a major affliction here could also affect judgement.

2. For a major event there must be appropriate symbolism shown in the progressed and directed chart of the person central to the event. Major transiting planets should also express proper symbolism. At least one of the personal points should be in close aspect to another personal point. If the natal chart doesn't show the possibility of a certain event at a given time, a suitable election will be difficult, if not impossible, to come by.

In early 1978 my natal progressed Ascendant came to the trine of the natal Midheaven. At the same time Neptune came to the trine of Mercury by solar arc direction in longitude. Three major transiting planets were aspecting my natal chart during this period; Saturn in conjunction with the Ascendant, Uranus opposite the Midheaven, and Jupiter conjunct the ruler of the 3rd house. These are appropriate background tones on which to build a major project, particularly a long term writing project.

3. In selecting the actual date on which to commence an event, attention should be paid to both the relationships of the transiting planets to themselves and to the natal chart of the central person. Probably the single most important concept to apply in examining the positions of the planets to themselves is that conditions be on the upswing. The "void of course" effect which a planet or an angle tends to exhibit when it is about to change signs should be avoided. This condition should never be happening to the significator of the event, nor should this planet be retrograde unless this is a repeat event. It is especially important to elect a time in which no major affliction will form among any two or more planets soon after the event is to begin. While hard aspects are necessary for energy and push, an early crisis in an event can often be more devastating than one several years down the road.

A second general concept to keep in mind is that the electional chart should always contain appropriate symbolism of the event. If the event is one in which crisis conditions are appropriate, perhaps close, hard aspects in the chart would be appropriate. In every case the significator(s) should be strong and unobstructed or the purpose and basic nature of the project will suffer. Favorable aspects from the significator or any other important point in the chart to the degree of a recent eclipse of planetary station are desirable.

The selection of the actual day on which to start actively writing was chosen on the basis of several considerations. The Sun just entering Aries, and a conjunction of Mercury and Venus in trine to Neptune around that time, drew my attention to the days around March 21st. A series of test charts were cast for March 21st and 22nd and it was decided to go with the 22nd as the Moon on the 21st would be in conjunction with Saturn, too much of an impediment for that body. The Moon would still be increasing in light at this point also. Several more test charts were cast, and after much juggling, chart 16 was arrived at, one in which many traditional rules were in effect. The symbolism is good, Jupiter being exactly rising in Gemini and in sextile to Saturn in the 3rd house. Mercury, the significator, is trine Neptune and conjunct Venus and is also in opposition to Pluto and square to Mars which giving it some "push" as the conjunction to Venus could indicate laziness. Mercury is also opposite the degree of the previous Solar eclipse and conjunct the degree of the next Solar eclipse two weeks ahead. The ruler of the 3rd house, the Sun, is strong in the 10th and is in close hard aspect to Uranus, the ruler of the 9th. Publishing would be a forced situation.

4. The electional chart must be compatible with the natal chart of the central person or persons involved with the event.

Comparison of this electional chart with my natal chart shows that the Sun is opposed to my natal 9th house ruler and the Moon is exactly quintile my natal 3rd house ruler. Mercury and Venus are trine natal Jupiter and the Moon is also sextile natal Mercury. The electional chart's Ascendant and Jupiter are conjunct my natal 3rd house ruler and the Midheaven is exactly positioned at the midpoint of my natal Midheaven and Jupiter.

134 / The Timing of Events: Electional Astrology

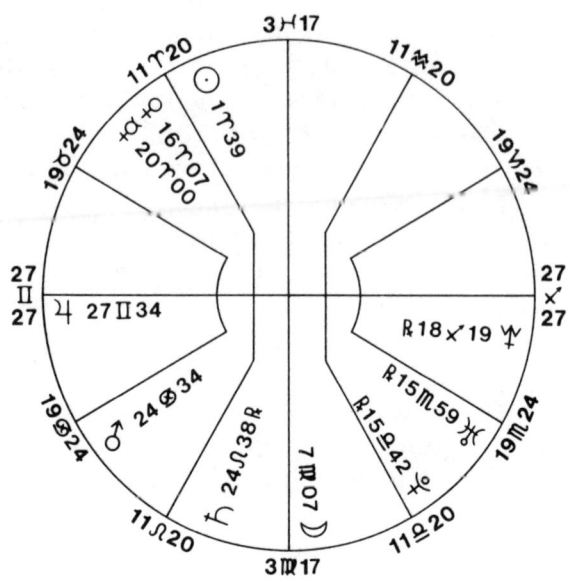

Chart 16

	Longitude	Latitude	Right Ascension	Declination
Sun	1°AR39'	0°N00'	1° 31'	0°N40'
Moon	7°VI07'	2°S33'	157° 53'	6°N32'
Mercury	20°AR00'	2°N01'	17° 42'	9°N41'
Venus	16°AR07'	0°S58'	15° 13'	5°N27'
Mars	24°CN34'	3°N03'	117° 05'	24°N12'
Jupiter	27°GE34'	0°S02'	87° 20'	23°N23'
Saturn	24°LE38' ℞	1°N33'	147° 28'	14°N47'
Uranus	15°SC59' ℞	0°N24'	223° 38'	16°S14'
Neptune	18°SG19' ℞	1°N28'	257° 26'	21°S28'
Pluto	15°LI42' ℞	17°N38'	201° 16'	10°N06'

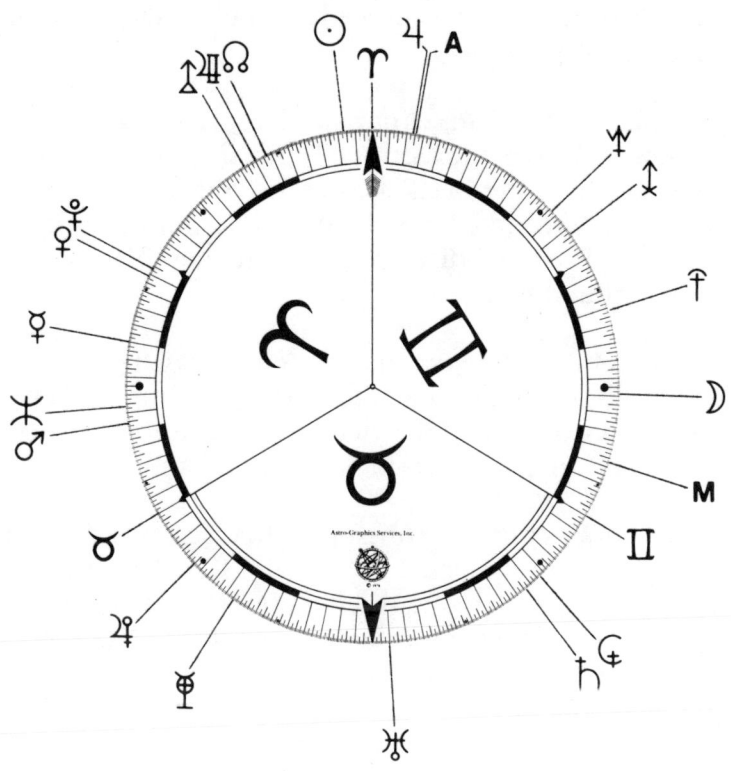

	Longitude	Latitude	Right Ascension	Declination
N. Node	6°LI17′	0°N00′	185° 46′	2°S30′
Cupido	3°SC35′ ℞	1°N06′	211° 43′	11°S41′
Hades	25°TA41′	1°S00′	53° 36′	18°N13′
Zeus	16°VI43′ ℞	0°N00′	167° 46′	5°N15′
Kronos	11°GE53′	0°N00′	70° 23′	22°N13′
Apollon	7°LI00′ ℞	0°N00′	186° 25′	2°S47′
Admetos	6°TA33′	0°N00′	34° 14′	13°N42′
Vulcanus	7°CN43′ ℞	0°N00′	98° 25′	23°N13′
Poseidon	23°LI39′ ℞	0°N00′	201° 54′	9°S11′
Ascendant	27°GE27′	0°N00′	87° 14′	23°N25′
Midheaven	3°PI17′	0°N00′	335° 12′	10°S18′

5. The electional chart should emphasize by angularity strong positive planets and should deemphasize, through placement in succeedent and cadent houses, problematic planets.

In chart 16 the Sun, strong in Aries, is angular in the 10th house. Jupiter is exactly conjunct the Ascendant and the Moon is strong in its own house, the 4th. No other planets are angular. Mars, Uranus, and Saturn express their energies in less direct ways due to their placements in background houses.

6. By carefully following the development of the event in relation to its elected chart, the timing of future actions can be determined and the meaning of the present can be understood through astrological symbolism.

The history of this writing project is clearly indicated by transits to its elected chart. The first few days of writing were very productive, but after five days of work, I dropped the project until September of that same year. At this point I again worked for about five consecutive days and finally reached the turning point, the completed first draft, just as Saturn conjuncted the electional chart's Moon and Mercury opposed its Sun position. Nothing further happened until January of 1979 when I typed the existing manuscript. At this time transiting Mars was opposing the electional charts Mars, Mercury was square the Sun, and Venus was trine to the Midheaven. On March 3rd, with Mars conjunct the charts Midheaven and Mercury conjunct its Sun, I worked two full days on the manuscript. On May 24th several copies of this edited first draft were sent out to publishers in hopes of getting some criticism. At this time Saturn was stationary at 7 degrees of Virgo, exactly conjunct the chart's Moon.

Except for some "not interested" and "needs more

work" notices from publishers, nothing else happened in regard to this project and it wasn't until September of 1980 that I got back to working on it. At this time Saturn was squaring the Ascendant and Jupiter, and Mercury was opposing the Sun, both of which were appropriate symbols for a major re-writing. As Saturn opposed the electional chart's Sun I hired a typist to retype the new manuscript and promptly forgot about the entire project. In January 1981, I again sent out some copies to publishers and over the next few months got some favorable responses, some criticisms, and even some suggestions.

As Jupiter and Saturn simultaneously opposed the electional charts Sun from their stationary positions in May and June of 1981, the final version of the manuscript came into being and arrangements were made for publishing. The actual third rewriting and editing occurred when Mercury moved forward from its station conjunct the Ascendant in July of that year. After more delays (my editors Saturn squares the electional charts Ascendant and Jupiter) I decided to add some more material to the text. By May of 1983 these were completed.

The Timing of Events: Electional Astrology

Designed by Gary Christen
Composed by Bruce Scofield and Gary Christen with
Intergraphics, Inc. transmission typesetting
in the Aster family of typefaces
Cover designed by Dee Dee Shea
Chart illustrations by Bruce Scofield
Proofread by Gary Christen, Barry Orr and
Joanne Scofield
Paste-up by Dee Dee Shea and Gary Christen
Printed and Bound by Mitchell-Shear, Inc. using
60# Natural acid-free paper

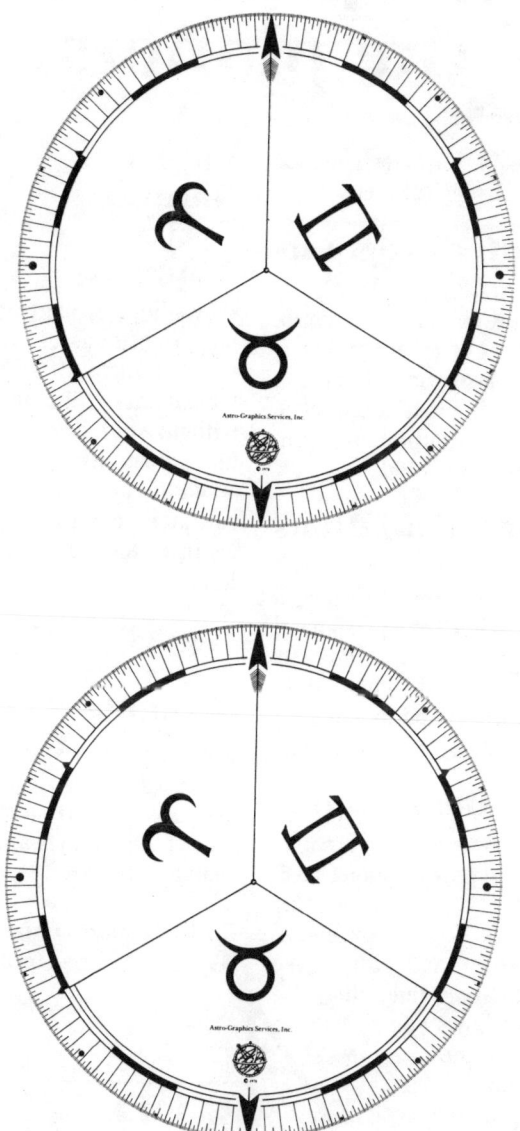

Keep track of the planets...

with Astrolabe's unique astrological tools.

Computer Programs

for your IBM, Apple, Macintosh, Commodore, Kaypro, Amiga or other computer. Over twenty programs, from our $50 Ancient Arts series to complete calculation and interpretation programs for less than $300.

Chart Calculations

Low-cost individual charts by mail. And many-paged chart analyses—natal readings, forecasts and compatibility reports—done by our own Electronic Astrologer™ programs.

Transit Graphs

that diagram a whole year of planet positions on one big 11" x 17" sheet. Geocentric 45-degree and 30-degree graphs. Declination and helio graphs. Each shows you instantly where the really important transits happen during the year, so you don't get lost in details.

Valliere's Natural Cycles Almanac

shows hour by hour planet positions as seen from your spot on earth. It tells when each planet rises, culminates, sets, etc., without your having to calculate a horoscope. Knowing these times when the planets are strongest, you can plan your life to run with, not against, the daily rhythm of the heavens.

Books, Dials, Press-On Symbols

and more! Space-age tools that give a more accurate perspective on the planets and help you do better astrology.

To learn more, write or phone for Astrolabe's free brochures.

NEW TOOLS FOR THE ANCIENT ARTS
ASTROLABE

DEPT. BR • BOX 28 • ORLEANS, MA 02653
TELEPHONE 1/617/255-0510